Healthy Dairy-free Eating

Mini C Tanya Carr RD RNutr

Allergy UK

Healthy Dairy-free Eating

photography by Martin Brigdale

angus

This book is dedicated to all members of my family, especially my mother and my loving son, Timothy. Their eternal support, encouragement and even criticism have been second to none. (Mini C)

For my wonderful Mum and Dad, two of my greatest teachers and friends, with much love. (Tanya Carr)

Acknowledgements

Mini C: Thanks to my mother, Surapee Mudita Karnasuta, who taught me to aim high but always to keep my feet on the ground. With her endless love and sacrifices I have come to realise that great achievements always come from within when you know in your heart that you have your loved ones all the way behind you. I would also like to give special thanks to my nanny, Sunee, who is in her mid-80s, and who was the first chef at our restaurant, the Busabong, to show me the most traditional and complicated methods in Thai cooking. Without this awareness, I would not have been able to create and adapt recipes for today's hectic lifestyle that also have authentic tastes and textures. I would like to thank all my friends who gave me great advice and to the brave ones that made a real sacrifice to be my guinea pigs – you could say my recipes have been tried and tested! I would also like to thank God for giving me a chance to spend more than half of my life abroad. If not for this, I would not have had the chance to become familiar with western and other foreign dishes and learn to cook them the way I have!

Tanya Carr: Thanks to my family, friends and colleagues for all for their ongoing help and encouragement and particular thanks to my fab sisters, Zoë and Heather – such blessings in my life. A very special thank you to my darling husband Shalom, for his encouragement, humour and love and for Eli, our scrumptious phlegmatic son, born in the middle of writing this book. Lastly a big thank you to Jenny, Muna, Ana and Ruth at Kyle Cathie – what a recipe for success – you are such pros and all so lovely with it!

Important note

This book is meant to be used as a general reference and recipe book. While the authors believe that the information and recipes it contains are beneficial to health, the book is in no way intended to replace medical advice. You should consult your doctor about specific medical issues.

Foreword by Allergy UK

Food allergy and intolerance is a huge problem in the UK, with in excess of 45 per cent of us suffering with such a condition. For those who have either been officially diagnosed by their GP or clinic or for those who suspect they may have a condition, it can be difficult to know where to start. It's like most things in life: until you know, you don't know and the unknown can be very frustrating!

At Allergy UK we represent the views and needs of people with allergy, food intolerance and chemical sensitivity. We provide up-to-date information, advice and support to help you with your allergy or intolerance. Our information fact sheets are written by allergy specialists and are updated every year, and along with the other support we provide will enable you to manage your condition as best as possible. Our network of nationwide support contacts are fellow sufferers and can assist you with the day-to-day practicalities of managing food allergy and intolerance. We also have a range of information available on our website. Regular newsletters keep you up to date with developments and we also run training for healthcare professionals. Our training is conducted by masters in their field and is provided to other healthcare professionals, thus raising the profile and understanding of this very big problem.

Having books available such as this one is important for food allergy and intolerance sufferers to provide further help and guidance, not to mention practical recipes. This is a user-friendly book and will appeal to a wide range of people, from the experienced allergy or intolerance sufferer to the newly diagnosed, or even those who only suspect they have a problem.

All aspects of a dairy-free diet are covered and are explained in great, easy-to-read detail. There are also practical tips throughout, including an example of how to keep a food and symptom diary. There are lots of recipes for all tastes and occasions and each recipe has an interesting introduction which makes it sound scrumptious and encourages you to make it.

Enjoy!

Allergy UK
www.allergyuk.org
Telephone: 01322 619 898

Why Go Dairy-free?

Nowadays, more and more people are turning to a dairy-free diet. But why, and what does dairy-free actually mean? Just a few years ago, if someone said they were choosing dairy-free, it would generally imply that their dietary intake was completely free from all dairy foods. They might have made this choice because of an intolerance to cow's milk, or for religious reasons, or for moral reasons such as being a vegan. However, today many more people are including dairy-free options in their diet and reducing their dairy intake for health and taste benefits, rather than avoiding dairy altogether for any other reason.

Health benefits?

One of the most popular and nutritionally sound alternatives to dairy is soya. Soya foods have received unprecedented attention in the press in the last couple of years largely because of their health benefits but also because of their vastly improved taste. This has undoubtedly fuelled the heightened interest in dairy-free. In countries where soya foods are eaten regularly there appears to be less risk of developing diseases such as heart disease and cancer, and in women certain symptoms of the menopause are reduced. Much research is currently being conducted into this.

Another reason why people are reducing dairy is its naturally occurring high saturated-fat content. A diet high in saturated fat increases the risk of raised blood cholesterol and heart disease – and many of us eat far more of this fat than we need. Numerous health campaigns have focused on the importance of watching our intake of saturated fat, the richest sources of which are meat and dairy produce. Now, instead of always opting for lower-fat meat and dairy products, people are seeking new tastes and more variety, regularly substituting dairy and meat with low-saturated-fat alternatives such as soya.

Cow's milk protein allergy, lactose intolerance and dairy reaction – what's the difference?

It can all seem confusing at times, but there are distinct differences between these three types of milk intolerance, each showing different symptoms and requiring a different method of diagnosis. They are summarised in the diagram below.

The most recently talked about intolerance has become known as 'dairy reaction'. This is different from the commonly recognised lactose intolerance and cow's milk protein allergy and is championed by some alternative

DAIRY INTOLERANCE

COW'S MILK PROTEIN ALLERGY

The immune system is reacting abnormally to dairy protein

LACTOSE INTOLERANCE

The gut is lacking the enzyme lactase which helps break down lactose (the sugar in milk)

DAIRY REACTION

Not fully understood or medically recognised, but there are some reports that symptoms of certain conditions, such as arthritis, headaches, general fatigue and irritable bowel syndrome, may be aggravated by dairy practitioners who believe that symptoms of conditions such as arthritis, headaches, general fatigue, irritable bowel syndrome (IBS), attention deficit disorder (ADD), attention deficit hyperactivity disorder (ADHD) and autism may be aggravated by dairy foods. Dairy reaction is not fully recognised by mainstream health professionals, although support and guidance are offered if individuals are obviously reacting to dairy.

In respect of ADD and ADHD in particular, there have been a number of case reports highlighting improvements in symptoms in a small number of children following a dairy-free diet. This of course does not apply to all children with ADD and ADHD, as scientists do not fully understand the link: further research is needed. It is therefore important to seek advice from a registered dietitian, and if possible a registered paediatric dietitian if you suspect that your child may be reacting to dairy foods.

Be totally reassured that you do not have to compromise at all on taste, variety or pleasure in cooking and eating dairy-free. In fact, this should be seen as a new beginning – an opportunity to gain health benefits and balance and optimise your diet as well as to introduce new ingredients and try a wide range of tasty recipes.

This book is for all people who are interested in dairy-free: for those following a strict dairy-free diet, a reduced dairy-free diet or who are simply including more dairy-free options in their diet. It is designed to provide all the information, help and advice you need along with a rich variety of delicious dairy-free recipes for you, your family and your friends to enjoy.

Reasons why people choose dairy-free

- Milk protein allergy
- Lactose intolerance
  - inherited
  - as a result of a gut infection and antibiotic use
  - as a result of gut surgery
  - as a result of a disease, such as coeliac disease, affecting the lining of the gut
  - as a result of malnutrition
- Religious reasons
- Moral reasons, such as veganism
- Dairy reaction – in some people symptoms associated with various conditions such as headaches, arthritis, IBS, eczema, autism, ADD and ADHD are aggravated by dairy
- Seeking a healthier lifestyle

What is Lactose Intolerance?

Lactose is a natural sugar found in human milk and the milk of other mammals, including goats and sheep. Lactose intolerance is not an allergic reaction. It occurs because the body lacks or produces an insufficient amount of an enzyme in our gut (intestines) called lactase.

Symptoms

During normal digestion, the lactase enzyme breaks down lactose into simpler sugars – glucose and galactose – so that the body can absorb it. If the body fails to produce enough lactase, the lactose passes through the gut unprocessed into the lower gut where the naturally present bacteria feed on it, giving off gas and causing pain, bloating, flatulence and diarrhoea.

Who is affected by lactose intolerance?

Lactose intolerance is estimated to affect around two thirds of the world's population. This condition is usually inherited and is more common among adolescents and adults, but in rare cases a child is born without an ability to make lactase. Some races, particularly those from Southeast Asia and the Middle East, parts of Africa and India, are more susceptible to lactose intolerance because they do not normally drink milk after infancy, so the body stops producing the lactase enzyme. Some of these sufferers find they can tolerate a certain amount of milk and that if they persist with drinking milk on a regular basis, the body begins to produce the enzyme again and their problems are overcome. In northern Europe, where dairy products are commonly eaten, people are less likely to have reduced levels of the lactase enzyme.

Lactose intolerance can also be brought on temporarily by malnutrition, a gut infection, gut surgery or because a disease such as coeliac disease has damaged the lining of the gut.

How much milk causes symptoms?

The quantity of milk needed to cause symptoms varies widely. Some people with this intolerance can drink as much as a glass of milk a day without any problems and sometimes more. Others have to avoid it altogether. A doctor or registered dietitian or nutritionist will be able to advise you about your particular condition and it may be a case of trial and error to find out how much you can consume without reacting. Dairy products with a low lactose content, like hard cheese, butter and bio-yogurts, can often be eaten by people who are lactose intolerant without any side effects. Some can tolerate an amount of goat's and sheep's milk, although these also contain lactose and can provoke a reaction. However, all the recipes in this book are completely dairy-free, so that they are suitable for every level of intolerance. If some dairy can be tolerated, the recipes can be adapted.

Diagnosis

Lactose intolerance may simply be diagnosed following detailed questioning by a doctor. It can also be diagnosed via a controlled food challenge (see page 14). Your doctor may be able to arrange for a lactose intolerance test or a 'hydrogen breath test', which are other ways of detecting a lactose intolerance.

Foods containing lactose, including ingredients to watch for on food labels

- Cow's milk
- Goat's and sheep's milk
- Milk powder, milk solids
- Buttermilk
- Cheese, cheese powder, cheese flavouring
- Yogurt, live yogurt
- Fromage frais
- Butter and margarine (unless milk-free)
- Cream
- Ice cream
- Milk sugar
- Milk chocolate
- Lactose
- Hydrolysed casein
- Whey, whey protein, whey syrup sweetener
- Certain low-calorie sweeteners
- Some brands of monosodium glutamate (MSG)

Other sources of lactose

- Medicines
- Dietary supplements, such as vitamin and mineral capsules
- Some toothpastes

About Allergies

A food allergy is a more severe type of food intolerance where the immune system reacts abnormally to a food or food substance. Normally our immune system acts as a defence mechanism, protecting the body from harmful substances such as viruses and bacteria and thereby preventing ill health. In the allergic person there is a breakdown in the immune system, causing the body to react to a normally harmless substance.

A traditional allergic response involves immune-system antibodies, known as IgE, and this happens very fast. In someone who has a dairy allergy, the body's antibodies are released in response to proteins in milk and almost immediately this triggers the release of histamine, producing an itchy inflammation. High levels of IgE antibodies to common food proteins, such as those found in milk, are often predictive of later allergy to inhalants, such as dust and pollen.

Many different substances can cause an allergic reaction, which often makes it very difficult to pinpoint the offending substance. Certain foods, including milk and milk products, nuts, seeds, fish (especially shellfish), eggs and wheat, are among the most common suspects in cases of food intolerance and allergy. Symptoms can be mild to severe, from discomfort to illness and, in the most extreme cases, death. An extreme reaction is referred to as an anaphylactic reaction. This is life-threatening and is thankfully rare. If you or your child suffers from anaphylaxis, it is vital that you go to an allergy specialist clinic. It is also highly recommended that you get in touch with the Anaphylaxis Campaign for more detailed information (see page 140). It is important with all allergies to pinpoint which food or foods are causing the problem so that appropriate action can be taken. Depending on the severity of the situation, this can mean eating less of the offending food or removing it from the diet altogether, temporarily or permanently.

What causes allergies?

The causes of allergies are not yet properly understood. Much research is in progress investigating this complex and controversial subject. Allergies do appear to have a genetic link, so if there is a family history, children are more likely to suffer from an allergy, particularly if both parents have this disposition. In fact, the chances that a child will develop an allergy are two to five times greater if either or both parents have a history of allergies.

Are allergies on the increase?

The short answer to this question is yes, though allergies are also being reported and diagnosed more than in the past. Diagnosis is not straightforward, and cases may also go undetected and unrecorded, with sufferers simply accepting and living with the symptoms.

Increased press reports certainly seem to give the impression that food intolerance and allergy in particular is becoming more prevalent. This may be a consequence of twentieth-century living, increased air pollution, more sterile environments and more use of chemicals and pesticides. It has also been suggested that modern medicine has reduced our risk of infection so that our immune systems are not sufficiently challenged and, in genetically susceptible individuals, respond to ordinary harmless substances. However, we have little research to prove that this is the case.

A study recently published in the Lancet found that although 20 per cent of adults thought they had some sort of food allergy, testing showed that only 3 per cent actually did. The prevalence of proven IgE food allergy in young children is in the order of 1–3 per cent, and it is less in adults at about 1 per cent of the population. The proven prevalence of food intolerance in general is 5–8 per cent in children and 1–2 per cent in adults.

It may not be true that more of us have food intolerance but rather that those that do are no longer suffering in silence. We may be more informed, better at recognising symptoms and more willing to actively seek help to discover what the problem is and how to alleviate it. Coupled with this, many of us are much more aware of the effect that diet has on well-being.

Food allergy does not commonly develop for the first time in adults. An exception is a reaction to shellfish. This tends to develop in older people rather than children.

Can milk allergies be prevented?

A baby's digestive system is unable to cope with the composition of cow's milk, so it is recommended that regular cow's milk should not be introduced before a child is six months old. It is often when cow's milk is introduced, either as a modified formula milk or during weaning on to solid foods, that unpleasant symptoms arise. Some evidence suggests that exclusive breastfeeding for up to six months may offer some protection against cow's milk intolerance.

Cow's milk protein allergy

Milk allergy is an immune reaction to the protein (not the lactose) found in milk. Unlike lactose intolerance, it is uncommon. It is generally restricted to young children and nearly always develops following the introduction of formula milk into their diet. Symptoms include vomiting, diarrhoea and abdominal pain, as well as problems involving the skin, such as eczema, and breathing. In rare cases the reaction can be severe. It affects about 3–5 per cent of children and usually clears up by the age of five years.

Once cow's milk protein allergy has been diagnosed (see page 14), a complete dairy-free diet is recommended until such time that dairy may be reintroduced as recommended by the doctor or registered dietitian.

Sometimes children suffer from both milk allergy and lactose intolerance. This can occur particularly after a gut upset.

Diagnosis of Dairy Intolerances

If you suspect that you have a milk (or any other) intolerance the first step is to visit your family doctor to ensure that your symptoms are not due to any other condition or illness. It really helps to take a food and symptom diary along with you (see right). A detailed examination of your general health, medical history and food diary can lead to a diagnosis, but some tests may be recommended to confirm a diagnosis or investigate a possible diagnosis.

The medical profession varies in its attitude and approach to the treatment of allergies. You may be referred to a specialist unit or clinic for tests or referred to a registered specialist dietitian if dietary changes are considered.

A word on 'dairy reaction'

Dairy reaction (see page 9) has a different effect on the body from that of lactose intolerance and cow's milk protein allergy. Instead of centering on IgE antibodies, it is identified by the presence of an antibody known as IgG which appears in days rather than minutes and may well have the wide-ranging effects that sufferers claim. There is a variety of tests for this type of milk intolerance, the most common involving testing a pinprick of blood for IgG responses to a range of food proteins, including those found in milk. The tests are not as yet fully recognised by mainstream medicine as the supporting scientific evidence is limited, but future research may highlight the benefits of IgG testing.

Recognised tests for allergies and intolerances

While the following tests are the most reliable ones currently available, most are not foolproof. It is often a combination of tests alongside the interpretation and advice of a skilled health professional that can lead to the best diagnosis.

The radio allergo sorbent test (RAST)

This test can be used for identifying acute allergies when there is an immediate reaction, by measuring IgE antibodies in the blood.

The skin-prick test

A few drops of a suspect allergen are put on the skin which is then pricked, so that the allergen seeps underneath. After a brief delay the doctor looks for signs of a reaction. This test is more successful for detecting environmental allergens, such as cat or dog hair which provoke an immediate reaction, and can be less useful for food allergies to which the reaction is often delayed.

Lactose tolerance test and hydrogen breath test

These can be used to confirm diagnosis of lactose intolerance. The lactose tolerance test measures the influence of lactose consumption on blood sugar levels, which can increase slightly if the lactose is not entirely digested. The hydrogen breath test measures the exhaled hydrogen after lactose consumption and is the more commonly used of the two methods. Raised hydrogen levels indicate the presence of undigested lactose because the gut bacteria ferment the undigested lactose and produce hydrogen, which is transported by the blood and released in the exhaled breath.

Exclusion and challenge diets

These are the most accurate and effective means of pinpointing a food intolerance. The process is straightforward, although time-consuming. Suspect foods are excluded from the diet and then you wait to see if symptoms improve. The suspect foods are then gradually reintroduced to see if the symptoms return.

All exclusion diets should be carried out with the supervision of a registered dietitian or nutritionist to ensure a balanced intake and advise on any necessary supplementation. Lifestyles vary and people have different dietary and medical requirements. A registered dietitian will be able to provide advice that is tailored to a particular situation and will be able to answer any specific questions. Exclusion diets should never be attempted with children or if there is any risk or history of anaphylaxis (see page 12), unless under strict supervision.

Any exclusion diet must be followed for at least two weeks to see if there is a noticeable improvement. You need to stick to it faithfully and keep a food and symptom diary to record the results. It is best to choose a period when you have no social commitments and enough time to devote complete attention to what you are eating and drinking.

There are many ways of following an exclusion diet and the one chosen will depend on whether a single food is already suspected as the culprit or whether there is the potential of more.

It is important to fill the diary in throughout the day, as it is very hard to remember what was eaten after the event. Record absolutely everything eaten and drunk, including any medicines and supplements.

Simple exclusion diet

This type of diet involves excluding all sources of one type of food, such as milk and dairy products, for two to four weeks, and then assessing if there is any improvement.

Few foods/elimination diet

This type of diet is used when food intolerance is suspected but the culprits are unconfirmed and is generally appropriate when multiple food intolerance is suspected. It involves eating a very basic diet of only five to seven fresh foods, which are thought least likely to cause an allergic reaction, for a recommended period of time. Other foods are then gradually reintroduced one by one so that the offending foods can be identified when symptoms occur. This diet can be very restrictive, sometimes boring and time-consuming. However, it can be tremendously useful if multiple intolerances are suspected. The good news is that excluding just milk products need not be difficult, daunting or tedious. The recipes in this book will give you lots of delicious options for enjoyable and nutritious menus.

Top tips when embarking on an elimination diet

- Plan ahead and have the foods in the house that you need.
- Choose a time that is easiest from a social point of view.
- Fill in your food and symptom diary as you go.
- Make an appointment to see your doctor and dietitian as soon as the diary is complete so that the experience is fresh in your mind.

If you are diagnosed with a cow's milk allergy, you will have to follow a completely dairy-free diet.

Non-medical-based allergy testing

Many places, including health-food stores, offer a variety of so-called allergy testing methods. These include hair analysis, pulse tests, sweat tests and kinesiology. However, they are unreliable and not recognised by the medical profession as having any scientific basis. They cost money and unfortunately result in many people unnecessarily following a complete dairy-free diet without expert guidance, often putting their nutrient intake and health at risk. Such a diet should be undertaken only on the advice of a qualified health professional.

Example of a food and symptom diary

DATE	TIME	FOOD AND DRINK CONSUMED	SYMPTOMS	TIME WHEN SYMPTOMS EXPERIENCED	SEVERITY RATING*
5 Jan	7am	Porridge with milk	Stomach cramps		
		Orange juice	and diarrhoea	9am	3
			Feeling tired	All morning	4

* Rate your symptoms as follows: 1=mild, 2=moderate, 3=bad, 4=severe.

Dairy-free and Nutrition

What exactly are dairy foods?

Dairy foods include cow's milk and any food that is derived from it, such as cheese, cream, butter and related items like buttermilk, yogurt, fromage frais and dairy ice cream. People following a dairy-free diet may or may not also have to avoid goat's and sheep's milk depending on whether they are intolerant to these. Dairy is in many more foods than may at first be apparent – numerous processed foods contain milk and dairy products. Obvious examples include spreads and chocolate, but there are many more. A detailed list along with top tips and advice about what to look for on food labels is found on pages 22–23. The recipes in this book are all free from cow's, goat's and sheep's milk and related products.

Is it healthy to avoid dairy?

Anyone wanting to start a strict dairy-free diet or even substantially reduce their dairy intake should first seek advice from a doctor or registered dietitian or nutritionist. Milk is one of the major foods in our diet, providing valuable amounts of protein, fat and carbohydrate as well as vitamins and minerals. It is a particularly good source of vitamins D, A and B2, is rich in calcium and a good source of phosphorus. For young children, milk is often a main provider of energy. If you give up dairy, it is therefore important to look at other ways of obtaining these nutrients, especially calcium.

There are alternative sources of all the nutrients that milk provides. Calcium is certainly one we should all focus on if significantly removing dairy from the diet. Some of us may also need to think about alternative protein sources, but the other nutrients should not pose problems for most people as long as they follow a varied diet. See page 28 for advice about a balanced intake. If you are unsure about certain nutrients, you should see a registered dietitian or nutritionist.

Why think about calcium?

Calcium is essential for healthy bones – it helps to give them their strength and density. Osteoporosis occurs when bones have lost so much of their mineral content that they become brittle and break easily. As dairy products are the main source of calcium in our diet, it is essential to replace this calcium if dairy is being significantly reduced or completely avoided.

Calcium is vital for young children and teenagers, but even after we stop growing at eighteen years, it remains very important in the diet. During pregnancy women should ensure that they are having enough calcium, and when breastfeeding they need extra.

Top tips for a good calcium intake and healthy bones

- Enjoy a balanced diet providing a wide range of nutrients.
- Get enough calcium: choose two or three servings of calcium-enriched dairy alternatives a day. Include other

Calcium content of various foods

Food	Calcium
200ml (7fl oz) glass whole/semi-skimmed/skimmed milk	237/248/249mg
200ml (7fl oz) glass calcium-enriched soya milk	240–280mg
200ml (7fl oz) glass calcium-fortified orange juice	245mg
Small tub (112g/4oz) cottage cheese	82mg
30g (1¼oz) hard cheese	216mg
Small tub (150g/5oz) low-fat yogurt	175mg
Small tub (120g/4¼oz) low-fat calcium-enriched soya yogurt	150mg
2 slices white/wholemeal bread	66/33mg
100g (3½oz) tinned sardines with bones	460mg
1 orange	72mg
150g (5oz) tin baked beans	80mg
12 almonds	62mg
2 tablespoons cooked spinach (90g/3¼oz)	128mg

good sources such as greens, dairy-free bread, and tinned fish with bones such as sardines. Some people need a supplement – but seek advice from a registered dietitian or nutritionist.

- Get enough vitamin D which helps with the absorption of calcium.
- Every day eat at least five portions of fruit and vegetables to supply you with potassium and other minerals which are also important for good bone health.
- When drinking alchohol, keep to sensible limits (see page 30).
- Stay active on a regular basis. Weight-bearing exercise (such as brisk walking, dancing and aerobics) is particularly beneficial for optimum bone health.

Calcium requirements

Age	Calcium (mg/day)
Children	
0–12 months	525
1–3 years	350
4–6 years	450
7–10 years	550
Males	
11–18 years	1,000
19 years +	700
Females	
11–18 years	800
19 years +	700
Breastfeeding	Extra 550

Should I worry about protein?

The protein ordinarily obtained from milk and milk products such as cheese and yogurt can easily be obtained from other foods. Such foods include soya milk and soya products, poultry, fish, nuts, legumes (peas, beans and lentils) and a combination of whole grains and vegetables. Only people who cannot take soya substitutes and have a low intake of animal foods might be at risk of insufficient protein in their diet. This can lead to poor growth development and repair of cells and could happen when, for example, someone was using rice milk instead of cow's milk because they were allergic to soya and were also vegetarian. People in this situation should most certainly seek guidance from a registered dietitian and nutritionist who will be able to ensure a balanced intake and assess whether any supplementation may be necessary.

How much protein do we need per day?

The amount of protein needed in the daily diet varies according to age and sex. Generally adults require 45–53g per day. See the table on page 19 as a guide to the protein content of various foods, to give you an indication of how these protein needs can be met.

Protein content of various foods

100g (3½oz) skinless chicken breast, grilled = 32g

250ml (9fl oz) glass semi-skimmed cow's milk = 8.2g

250ml (9fl oz) glass low-fat soya milk = 9.3g

Rice milk = 0.0g

1 medium slice granary bread = 3.4g

1 medium slice white bread = 3g

12 almonds = 5.5g

180g (6½oz) white rice (cooked weight) = 4.7g

230g (8¼oz) macaroni (cooked weight) = 7g

60g/2¼oz (average portion) boiled carrots = 0.4g

What about vitamin D?

The body makes its own vitamin D when exposed to sunlight. This exposure is our main source of vitamin D. In northern countries it is recommended that you expose your skin to the daylight for 10–20 minutes every day between early spring and mid-autumn, but avoid sun exposure between the hours of 12pm and 3pm in the summer months.

In addition egg yolk and fish, particularly fish liver oils, are good sources of vitamin D. There are small quantities in carrots, pumpkins, sweet potatoes, apricots, squash, broccoli, spinach and other dark leafy greens.

Milk substitutes

Calcium-enriched soya milk and yogurt should ideally be the main substitutes for dairy milk and yogurt as they have the best nutrient profile. Soya's protein quality is equivalent to that of meat, milk and eggs, which are the main protein sources in our diet. Rice milk is normally advised for those who cannot take soya.

Generally speaking, as long as people choose calcium-enriched soya milks and yogurts for dairy products, they should not suffer from a nutritional point of view. If using rice milk, a calcium-enriched variety should be chosen and it is also important to ensure that there is enough protein in the diet. Rice milk provides little more than water and added calcium, so when using rice milk in a recipe, always include a good protein source such as meat or pulses.

Other cow's milk substitutes include nut milks, goat's and sheep's milk and lactose-reduced milks. However, their nutrient level may be much less than that of dairy or soya milks or they may contain a certain amount of lactose.

Adding soya to your shopping basket can benefit your health

- It has recently been recognised that eating soya foods on a regular basis helps to lower blood cholesterol. This is good news when we consider that seven out of ten adults in the UK have raised cholesterol levels that are significantly increasing their risk of coronary heart disease.
- Soya protein is the active cholesterol-lowering ingredient in the soya bean. It has been proved that consuming 25g (1oz) of soya protein a day as part of a low-saturated-fat diet will help to lower blood cholesterol.
- Achieving your 25g (1oz) daily intake of soya protein is easy. Simply include two 250ml (9fl oz) glasses of soya milk and a 200g (7oz) serving of soya yogurt as part of your daily low saturated-fat diet, or alternatively use tofu in a stir-fry and include 250ml of soya milk in a fruit smoothie or on your cereal and in tea throughout the day. Do note however that the amount of soya protein in soya cream is negligible.
- The recipes in this book which include soya have been labelled according to how much soya protein they contain, which can help you assess if you are having 25g (1oz) per day.
- Some women find that soya can help reduce unpleasant symptoms of the menopause. Those who suffer from severe hot flushes benefit the most.
- Soya is very nutritious and is one of the few sources of high-quality complete protein equivalent to that found in meat, dairy produce and eggs, making it a useful food for all the family.

- Soya products have significantly changed over the years. As a food choice these days they are not only healthy but a tasty food too – far removed from some of the strange options that were available in the past. If you've never tried soya products before or haven't tasted them for a long time, then prepare to be pleasantly surprised!
- Including more soya in your diet follows eastern ways of eating in which dairy foods hardly feature. Indeed, around half of the recipes in this book have a Thai influence, but we have also included more traditional western-type dishes with soya milk substitutes for the usual dairy products.

Taste and availability of dairy-free

The greatly improved taste and increased availability of dairy alternatives have certainly made it easy and more enjoyable to include them in our daily diet. Several years ago these foods were mostly confined to health-food stores, with limited supplies found somewhere in the back of only a few supermarkets. Today they are available in all supermarkets and are highly visible alongside the dairy equivalents.

The increased popularity of dairy alternatives is reflected not only on the supermarket shelves but in restaurants and cafes too. When we ask for a cappuccino, we are now commonly given the choice of a soya or dairy-free version – something quite unheard of a couple of years ago.

Whatever the reason for omitting dairy from your meal or diet, one thing is for sure: you can still enjoy a wide range of varied and delicious meals.

Nutrient comparison of calcium-enriched soya milk and semi-skimmed cow's milk

NUTRITION PER 100ML (3½FL OZ)	CALCIUM-ENRICHED SOYA MILK	SEMI-SKIMMED COW'S MILK
Kcal	47	47
Protein	3.8g	3.4g
Fat	2.2g	1.7g
Saturated	0.4g	1.1g
Polyunsaturated	1.4g	0g
Monounsaturated	0.5g	0.4g
Essential fatty acids		
Linoleic acid	58%	0%
Alpha linolenic acid	8%	0%
Carbohydrates	2.8g	5.2g
Lactose	0g	5.2g
Cholesterol	0g	7mg
Calcium	120–140mg	124mg

Dairy Foods to Avoid

Depending on how strict your dairy-free diet needs to be, it may be necessary to avoid all of the following foods and ingredients or just some of them. Always check the labels carefully as products vary from brand to brand.

Dairy foods

- Fresh cow's milk – skimmed, semi-skimmed and whole
- Tinned condensed, evaporated and powdered cow's milk
- Buttermilk
- Cream
- Fromage frais
- Crème fraîche
- Quark
- Butter
- Cheese
- Yogurt
- Ice cream

Processed foods that may contain dairy

Many people do not realise how many foods actually contain quantities of dairy – chocolate is one and it is easy to underestimate how much dairy you are really eating.

Vegetables

- Vegetables tinned in sauce containing milk or milk products: for example, creamed sweetcorn
- Instant mashed potato

Bread and baked goods

- Most bread
- Most biscuits
- Some crackers
- Doughnuts
- Scones
- Many cakes
- Many baking mixes

Cereals and grains

- Most types of muesli and many breakfast cereals now contain some dairy ingredient, particularly skimmed milk powder

Confectionery and snack foods

- Milk chocolate and some plain chocolate
- Fudge
- Toffee
- Butterscotch
- Many other sweets
- Roasted nuts with a lactose-containing flavouring or milk-chocolate covering
- A number of potato crisp brands, especially flavoured varieties

Desserts

- Most instant desserts
- Most traditional pudding types
- Tinned rice pudding
- Batter mixes and pancakes
- Cheesecakes
- Mousses
- Custards

Savoury foods

- Many soups
- Creamy sauces
- Dips based on yogurt, fromage frais or cheese
- Salad dressings made with milk or milk products
- Certain shop-bought gravies
- Quiches and flans
- Many ready meals
- Crumbed and battered foods
- Yorkshire puddings
- Some sausages and other processed meats: for example, some hams
- Some pies, sausage rolls and pastries
- Pizzas
- Lasagnes
- Many pasta dishes
- Some waffles

Beverages

- Coffee whitener
- Milkshakes
- Many fruit smoothie drinks
- Malted milk drinks, such as Horlicks, Ovaltine and Bournvita
- Vending-machine tea
- Instant hot chocolate drinks (cocoa is usually dairy-free)
- Cream-based liqueurs and cocktails

Spreads, fats and oils

- Dairy spreads
- Most brands of margarine contain some buttermilk, skimmed milk or whey powder
- Low- or reduced-fat spreads can contain buttermilk
- Most lemon curd
- Chocolate spread

Miscellaneous

- Monosodium glutamate (the flavour enhancer) containing lactose
- Some stock cubes
- Tablets containing a lactose filler
- Toothpaste containing a lactose filler
- Low-calorie sweeteners containing lactose

Hidden dairy ingredients

Apart from the obvious dairy ingredients listed above, milk products appear in numerous guises in many processed foods, from batters to biscuits and margarines to medicines. For instance, cow's milk protein may be included in foods in the form of casein or whey and many people do not realise that these are derived from cow's milk. Watch out for the following terms in the lists of ingredients on food packaging.

Terms used by manufacturers that indicate the presence of cow's milk

- Butter listed as fat, flavouring, oil or solids
- Casein, hydrolysed casein, rennet casein
- Caseinates (ammonium, calcium, magnesium, potassium, sodium)
- Curds
- Dried milk (non-fat milk powder)
- Dry milk solids
- Hydrolysed milk protein
- Lactalbumin, lactalbumin phosphate
- Lactate
- Lactoferrin
- Lactoglobulin
- Lactose
- Milk derivative fat/solids
- Opta (fat replacer)
- Simplesse (fat replacer)
- Soured cream solids/milk solids
- Whey, delactosed whey, demineralised whey, sweet whey powder, whey powder, whey protein concentrate, whey solids

Food preparation and contamination

Depending on how strict your diet has to be, you may need to think about possible sources of contamination: for instance, having chips from a chip shop fried in oil which may have previously been used to fry a battered food; or eating non-dairy cheese from a cheeseboard shared with dairy cheese and cut with the same knife.

If you suffer from a severe food allergy it is important to gain specialist advice on food preparation and contamination from food allergy clinics as well as specialist organisations such as Allergy UK and the Anaphylaxis Campaign (see page 140 for details).

Traps for the unwary: foods in which it is not obvious that cow's milk may be present

Soya cheese
Goat's cheese
Vegetarian cheese
Margarine and low-fat spreads
Bread
Biscuits and cakes
Sausages
Rusks
Non-milk-fat ice cream
Instant mashed potato
Muesli and many breakfast cereals
Packet and tinned soups
Fish coated in batter

Dairy Alternatives

A totally dairy-free diet involves the complete avoidance of cow's, goat's and sheep's milk, milk products such as butter, cheese, cream and yogurt, milk derivatives such as casein, whey, hydrolysed whey and non-fat milk solids, and lactose (milk sugar). Lactose is found in many foods as well as being used by the pharmaceutical industry as a filler in some tablets. All dairy alternatives listed below are suitable for those with cow's milk protein allergy as well as lactose intolerance. Goat's and sheep's milk may be tolerated in the diet of some cases of cow's milk protein allergy, but because they also contain some lactose they are generally unsuitable for people with lactose intolerance.

Many supermarkets now regularly produce a list of milk-free manufactured foods. All supermarkets offer a customer service telephone number which you can ring for this kind of information but it must be remembered that this rapidly becomes out of date owing to changes in the formulation of foods and the introduction of new products.

Dairy-free foods

It is impossible to give a 'safe' list and so it is crucial always to check the ingredients on the packaging of manufactured brands of food for the presence of milk or milk derivatives. Below is a list of items that can generally be eaten safely (but still always read the label!) and it can be used as a general shopping list.

Fruit and vegetables

- Fruit (fresh, tinned and frozen)
- Fruit juices (fresh, frozen, tinned, bottled and UHT)
- Vegetables (fresh, frozen, dried)
- Certain brands of tinned baked beans
- Certain brands of instant mashed potato

Meat and meat alternatives

- Fresh meat, poultry, game, bacon and offal – not processed
- Most burgers, rissoles and sausages – but check the label

Fish and fish products

- Fresh or frozen fish without batter or crumb coating
- Tinned fish in brine, oil or water
- Smoked plain fish
- Certain brands of fish fingers

Bread and baked goods

- Certain pitta breads, muffins and bagels – check the ingredients
- Some pastries and fruit pies – check the ingredients
- Meringues
- Homemade cakes and biscuits made with milk-free ingredients and certain bought brands – check the ingredients

Baking ingredients

- Baking powder
- Fresh and dried yeast
- Most flours
- Certain brands of blancmange power
- Certain brands of custard powder
- Most plain dark chocolate
- Desiccated coconut
- Dried fruit
- Pastry – if made with pure vegetable fat
- Marzipan
- Mincemeat

Cereals and grains

- Porridge oats
- Certain brands of breakfast cereal such as Rice Krispies, some cornflakes (plain), Shreddies (plain), Weetabix
- Pasta, macaroni, rice and other grains such as couscous, bulgar wheat

Confectionery, preserves and snack foods

- Some plain chocolates, jellies and boiled sweets
- Carob
- Sugar, glucose, jam, honey, treacle, marmalade and certain brands of lemon curd
- Plain ice lollies, most sorbets and most jellies
- Nuts
- Pretzels
- Some potato crisps
- Most cream crackers and water biscuits
- Some oatcakes, rice cakes and crispbreads

Soups

- Minestrone, lentil, oxtail, vegetable and French onion – but check the ingredients

Sauces

- Mustard
- Some soy sauces
- Most tomato ketchups and purées
- Most relishes and chutneys
- Certain brands of gravy granules

Dips

- Hummus
- Fresh tomato salsa

Beverages

- Fresh fruit juices
- The majority of soft drinks – but check the ingredients
- Tea
- Coffee
- Cocoa
- Certain brands of drinking chocolate
- Certain squashes and most fizzy drinks
- Wines, spirits and beers (caution should be taken with some liqueurs and cocktails)

Spreads, fats and oils

- Vegan margarine, pure soya spread, kosher margarine, beef and vegetable suet
- All pure vegetable and nut oils
- French dressing, mayonnaise and salad cream
- Most brands of peanut butter

Miscellaneous

- Salt
- Pepper
- Herbs and spices
- Vinegar
- Bovril
- Marmite

Milk and dairy substitutes

A wide range of milk substitutes is now available in all supermarkets as well as health-food stores and many local convenience shops. These can be used to replace regular cow's milk in drinks, on cereals and in all recipes.

A form of cow's milk that may be tolerated

Lactose-reduced milk is made from cow's milk, but has a reduced lactose content through the addition of a natural lactase enzyme, similar to that found in our digestive system. This milk is available in long-life form and is generally a full-fat product. It can be used by people with lactose intolerance who can tolerate some dairy.

Soya milks and soya drinks

Soya milk is the obvious choice for most people as a substitute for cow's milk – unless they are also allergic to soya protein. Made from soya beans, soya milk is widely available freshly chilled or in long-life form, sweetened or unsweetened, and in various flavours. It is more often than not fortified with calcium. It may also have some added vitamins. Soya drinks are lactose-free, cow's milk protein free and generally low in fat with an equivalent fat content to that of semi-skimmed cow's milk, although more rarely some fat-free and full-fat versions are available. The plain sweetened options are sweetened to the level of cow's milk, and are therefore easily accepted by the palate when you are first making the switch. However, in the long run, it is worth considering the unsweetened options, as they will be kinder to your dental health.

Plain soya milk can be used as a complete milk replacement on cereals as well as in hot drinks such as tea and cappuccino and in all kinds of recipes. Surprisingly it has a more creamy flavour than semi-skimmed cow's milk even though it is low in fat. No soya milk to date can be used with regular coffee as it tends to curdle.

Approximately 80 per cent of people allergic to cow's milk can tolerate soya, but some allergic individuals may react to soya protein as well as to goat's and sheep's milk protein.

Regular soya milks should not be introduced as a main milk source for children under two years of age. Calcium-enriched varieties can be used from six months in cooking but not as a main milk source.

Coconut milk and cream

Coconut milk makes a tasty substitute for dairy in many recipes and goes particularly well in Thai dishes including the ones in this book. However, it is one of the few vegetable foods that is high in saturated fat – the type of fat more commonly found to be high in animal foods such as full fat milk and cheese – and we should all be having less of it. Try not to use coconut milk too often and dilute with water or use the reduced-fat version if you want to lower the fat content but keep the taste.

Goat's and sheep's milk

Both goat's and sheep's milk contain lactose and so are unsuitable for anyone with more than a mild intolerance to lactose. These types of milk can also provoke a reaction in allergic individuals. Their protein content is similar to that of cow's milk, though not identical. Goat's milk is deficient in folic acid, so if it is chosen regularly the user should ensure a good intake of folic acid from other sources including green leafy vegetables and wholemeal foods.

Goat's and sheep's milk are both as versatile as cow's milk. Goat's milk has a much stronger taste than cow's milk and sheep's milk has a higher fat content, which makes it taste creamier and richer. It also sweeter than cow's milk.

These milks are not recommended for children under 2 years as a main milk source.

Rice milk

Rice milk is generally made from filtered water, rice syrup, vegetable oil and various flavourings. Some types now have added calcium as it otherwise contains no calcium. It is lactose-free, low in fat and contains a negligible or very small amount of protein.

Oat drink

Usually made from whole oats, vegetable oil and filtered water, oat drink is lactose-free, low in fat and contains a negligible or very small amount of protein.

Yogurts, desserts and ice cream

Regular cow's yogurt is a fermented milk food which may contain bacteria with enzymes that can digest the lactose in milk to produce lactic acid. It is therefore lower in lactose than milk and may be tolerated by people with mild lactose intolerance.

If goat's or sheep's milk can be tolerated by those with mild lactose intolerance, yogurts made from these milks are an option. They can now be found in some of the larger supermarkets and health-food stores.

For people requiring a completely dairy-free alternative, there is a wide range of tasty soya yogurts, desserts and ice cream available.

Creams

Soya cream is widely obtainable as a long-life alternative to single dairy cream from supermarkets and health-food stores.

Goat's cream is available from larger supermarkets and health-food stores. It has a sweet taste and can be used as a pouring or whipped cream in recipes.

Cheeses

Hard cheeses like Cheddar and Parmesan are relatively low in lactose, enabling small amounts to be tolerated by those with a mild lactose intolerance. There is a relatively widely available selection of good-tasting goat's and sheep's cheeses which can also be used easily in cooking. However, some brands can include cow's milk, so it is important to read the label. Alternatively there is a number of cheeses made from soya, mostly available from health-food stores. These are the only soya foods which to date do not tend to taste as good as their dairy counterparts – they are often rather mild and rubbery. They also tend not to melt in the same way as dairy cheese.

Fats and spreads

Vegetable margarines and spreads often contain some whey or buttermilk which is added for flavour but makes them unsuitable for a dairy-free diet. It is important to choose from the dairy-free soya spreads, kosher or vegan spreads or to use pure vegetable fats and oils. All can be used for spreading and in cooking.

Tofu

Tofu is a high-protein low-fat food made from soya beans. A fermented soya bean curd, it comes in a block which can have a firm or soft (silken) texture and is available plain, marinated or smoked. Tofu is a good source of calcium and protein and is extremely versatile: it can be used in a wide variety of dishes, both sweet and savoury. Silken tofu is creamy and good for dips, sauces and toppings. Firm tofu can be marinated and used instead of cheese or meat.

Choosing a Balanced Diet

Enjoying a balanced diet is important for everyone, which of course includes those following a dairy-free diet. Healthy food not only tastes good but it affects our mood and behaviour too, making us all feel better and more alert as well as boosting our energy levels. Eating healthily helps us all to get the most from life. Furthermore eating well reduces our risk of many health problems, including heart disease, diabetes and cancer.

A balanced diet should include a wide variety of foods from all five food groups every day. These are listed opposite in the table. Please note that this is a general guide and is not meant for children under five years of age, who have different dietary needs.

Fluid intake

Many of us do not think about our fluid consumption – it often takes second place to food. However, it is equally important. Around two thirds of the human body is made up of fluid. This is constantly lost or used up daily as we breathe, sweat and go to the toilet. If we have an insufficient fluid intake, we cannot concentrate 100 per cent and will not be as alert as we could be. We will also be increasing our chances of ill health as we will not be sufficiently clearing all the toxins from our body. Most people need at least 2 litres ($3^1/_2$ pints) of fluid a day – about 8 glasses – but more is required in hot weather and

Choosing healthy food from the five main groups

FOOD GROUP	MAIN NUTRIENTS PROVIDED	WHAT TO CHOOSE?	HOW MUCH?
Potatoes, rice, bread, cereals, pasta and other grains	Carbohydrate, fibre, B vitamins, potassium, some protein, some iron, some calcium, vitamin E, phytochemicals (natural plant elements)	Rice, potatoes, pasta, noodles, dairy-free crackers/bread, dairy-free breakfast cereals	5–14 portions daily **1 portion is:** 3 tablespoons breakfast cereal 1 slice bread/fruit bread/ mini pitta 1/2 bread roll/bun 1/2 scone/pancake/crumpet 2 egg-sized potatoes 3 tablespoons boiled pasta 2 heaped tablespoons boiled rice
Fruit and vegetables	Vitamin C, folic acid, potassium, fibre, beta carotene, some calcium, some iron, magnesium, some carbohydrate	All types – fresh, frozen, tinned, dried; fresh juices	5 or more daily **1 portion is:** 1 piece of regular fresh fruit e.g. 1 orange, 1 banana 2 small fruit, e.g. 2 kiwis, 2 plums 2 tablespoons stewed or tinned fruit 1 small glass (200ml/7fl oz) fruit juice 1 tablespoon dried fruit
Dairy alternatives	Calcium, protein, vitamins A, D, B2 and B12, zinc, phosphorus (phytochemicals in plant-based options)	Lower-fat versions: low-fat calcium-enriched soya milks and yogurts	2–3 portions daily **1 portion is:** 200ml (7fl oz) calcium-enriched dairy alternative 1 small tub (120g/4 1/4oz) calcium-enriched yogurt alternative 25g (1oz) dairy-free soya cheese
Meat, fish and alternatives	Protein, iron, zinc, magnesium, potassium (phytochemicals in peas, beans, lentils and tofu options), essential fats from fatty fish options	Lean meats, poultry, fish, eggs, beans, peas, lentils, nuts, meat substitutes	2–4 portions daily **1 portion is:** 50–70g (2–3oz) beef, pork, ham, lamb, liver, kidney, chicken, fish 2 eggs 5 tablespoons cooked beans (such as kidney or aduki) 4 tablespoons cooked lentils 2 tablespoons nuts
Foods rich in fat and/or sugar	Fat, including some essential fats, sugar, vitamins, minerals	Vegetable oils such as olive, rapeseed, soya and their spreads, low-fat dairy-free dressings	Eat in small amounts. Keep sugary foods and drinks to mealtimes to help reduce risk of tooth decay

when exercising. A good way of telling if you are drinking enough is to check the colour of your urine. It should be a light straw colour. If it is brown and smelly, you need to drink more.

Alcohol

Too much alcohol can damage the heart muscle, increase blood pressure and also lead to weight gain. However, a sensible amount of alcohol on a regular basis can be good for our health. The current daily recommended intake is no more than 2–3 units for women and 3–4 units for men. A unit is equivalent to:

- 300ml (1/2 pint) beer, lager, stout (such as Guiness), cider
- 1 small (125ml/4 1/2fl oz) glass of wine
- 25ml (just under 1fl oz) measure of spirits
- 50ml (2fl oz) glass of sherry or port

Avoid milky liqueurs and cocktails.

Salt

A certain amount of salt each day is essential, but it is important to watch our intake. Most of us eat far too much salt and our liking for it is all down to habit. As in the case of sugar, if we reduce our salt intake gradually our tastebuds will adapt. Salt intake should not exceed 6g per day, equivalent to 1 teaspoon. When cooking and at the table, try to limit the amount of salt you add, or skip it altogether. You will be surprised at how well your palate adjusts and how soon you won't like salty foods. When shopping and cooking, check food labels; if salt is listed as sodium, convert to grams of salt by multiplying the sodium value by 2.5.

And don't forget to keep moving...

With our sedentary lifestyles, most of us do not exercise nearly enough. This not only increases our chances of ill health but also affects our mood. It is amazing how a small amount of regular activity can change your outlook on life. It is currently recommended that every day we all do at least thirty minutes and up to one hour of activity or the equivalent of taking 10,000 steps! The key to regular exercise is to build up the habit.

Finally... get label happy!

Whatever type of diet you may be following (and if you are not following one but want to eat healthily), you need to watch your consumption of fat, sugar and salt. It is often confusing trying to determine which foods are low in fat, sugar and salt and also high in fibre. However, the simple guidelines below can make this assessment much easier.

For ready meals and foods you eat in large amounts, look at the amount of fat, sugar, sodium and fibre per serving listed. For snacks and foods you eat in small amounts, see the 'per 100g' information.

How many calories a day do I need?

The table below is a rough guide to the recommended daily amounts of calories and nutrients for an average man and woman. Use this information to help you make sense of food labels. For example, if a ready meal contains 50g (2oz) of fat, you know that it has over half the recommended amount of fat for the day.

Reading the ingredients label

If following a completely dairy-free diet, it is vital that you read the ingredients labels of all processed and convenience

How much is a lot?

A lot	A little
10g sugar	2g sugar
20g fat	3g fat
5g saturated fat	1g saturated fat
3g fibre	0.5g fibre
0.5g sodium	0.1g sodium
(or 1.25g salt)	(or 0.25g salt)

Recommended daily calorie and nutrient intake

	Men	Women
Energy (calories)	2,500kcals	2,000kcals
Sugar	70g	50g
Fat	95g	70g
of which saturates	30g	20g
Fibre	20g	16g
Sodium	2.5g	2g
(or salt)	7g	5g

foods before purchasing them. By law, food labels must list all the ingredients in order of weight and lists can be quite lengthy. It may seem time-consuming examining labels, but it becomes easier when you are only checking for any changes in the ingredients of foods you are already familiar with.

What if there is no label?

There is no legal requirement for loose unpackaged foods to have a list of ingredients. If you need to know more about such food products as bread fresh from the bakery, ask the shop assistant who should have access to a product information guide.

Product changes

Manufacturers change their ingredients from time to time to improve a recipe or because they have changed their supplier, so it's best not to assume that a product is safe to eat simply because you have bought it before – be sure to always check the label.

Example of an ingredients label from a typical brand of muesli (spot the dairy ingredients!)

INGREDIENTS
Whole wheat, rolled oats, raisins (12.5%), sugar, dried skimmed milk, dried milk whey, mixed sliced nuts (3%) (hazelnuts, almonds), malted barley extract, salt
CONTAINS: gluten, cow's milk, nuts

NUTRITION INFORMATION

	Per 40g serving	Per 100g serving
Energy	613 kJ 145kcal	1532kJ 362kcal
Protein	4.1g	10.3g
Carbohydrate	26.9g	67.2g
(of which sugars)	8.8g	21.9g
Fat	2.3g	5.8g
(of which saturates)	0.3g	0.8g
Fibre	2.8g	6.9g
(of which soluble)	0.7g	1.7g
(of which insoluble)	2.1g	5.2g
Sodium	0.07g	0.17g

These figures are recommended by nutrition professionals for average-weight adults. You should adjust your intake according to your own age, weight, build and lifestyle. This pack contains at least 37 servings.

Per 40g serving (4 heaped dessertspoonfuls)
145 calories 2.3g fat 0.17g salt

Guideline Daily Amounts

Each Day	Women	Men
Calories	2000	2500
Fat	70g	95g
Salt	5g	7g

Dairy-free Shopping and Cooking

Preparing for your first dairy-free shopping trip may seem daunting at first. However, with the wide variety of foods now available in supermarkets and the ever-increasing choice of dairy-free products, you will be surprised at how quickly you will adjust both to shopping and preparing your food.

To begin with use the list of dairy-free foods on page 25 as the basis for a good shopping list. All major supermarkets produce a list of their dairy-free branded foods which will also help with shopping and getting used to the foods you can safely enjoy. A number of supermarkets also have their own 'free from' range of foods where dairy-free foods may now be all found in one section. Many supermarkets have their own customer careline which you can phone for detailed information about products. Look out also for the manufacturer's careline number on label of branded foods (see Resources, page 140).

Changing your diet provides you with a great opportunity to focus on what you are eating, to go back to basics and follow a really healthy eating regime. Stock up on a wide variety of foods from all the major food groups as highlighted on page 29. Stock your fridge-freezer with fish, chicken, eggs, lean meat, fruit, fresh and frozen vegetables, and dairy-free alternatives to milk, yogurt, cheese and so on. It is important to have a plentiful supply of dairy-free drinks that you enjoy from water to tea, fruit juices and dairy-alternative milks (the calcium-enriched varieties). It might also be a good time, depending on how much you have cooked in the past, to think about healthy cooking equipment.

Healthy cooking equipment

- Non-stick pans
- Wok
- Steamer
- Pressure cooker
- Food processor
- Vegetable scrubber and peeler
- Juicer

Stocking your store cupboard

Use the following list to help you fill your store cupboard with healthy dairy-free ingredients:

- Dairy-free breakfast cereals such as porridge oats and Weetabix
- Fresh calcium-enriched soya milk and cream, soya cheese and yogurts
- Fresh vegetables e.g. sweet potatoes, peppers, broccoli, tomatoes, onions, aubergines, chillies, pumpkin, mangetout, carrots, spring onions, frozen peas
- Fresh fruit e.g. pears, apples, bananas, lemons, limes, lychees, mangoes
- Herbs e.g. coriander, mint, parsley
- Pasta, rice and noodles e.g. tagliatelle, macaroni, rice noodles, basmati rice, risotto rice
- Popping corn, plain nuts and seeds e.g. roasted peanuts, pine nuts, flaked almonds, walnuts, sesame seeds
- Wholemeal flour, plain white flour, rice flour
- Buckwheat, couscous, polenta
- Dried fruit: apricots, prunes, raisins and sultanas
- Tinned or dried beans, peas and lentils
- Tinned fruit in natural juice
- Tinned tomatoes, sweetcorn, bamboo shoots
- Tinned salmon, mackerel, tuna and sardines in brine
- Tofu
- Garlic, ginger, chillies, lemongrass, olives, vinegars, Thai fish sauce, dairy-free soy sauces – light and dark, dairy-free bottled tomato sauce and mustards, honey
- Spices e.g. chilli powder, curry paste, turmeric powder, cumin seeds, ground cinnamon
- Olive, groundnut, rapeseed, sesame and chilli oils
- Chicken, beef and vegetable stock cubes
- Ready-made long-life low-fat soya custard

Dairy-free cooking

Dairy substitutes such as soya milk can be used as a straight swap for cow's milk on cereals, in tea and in numerous recipes from sauces, soups and other savoury dishes to puddings and cakes. (See page 26 for more information). All the inspiration you need for healthy, dairy-free cooking is provided by the recipes later on in this book. They offer plenty of delicious options for the whole family and for every occasion.

Suggested menu plans for healthy dairy-free eating

	MENU 1	MENU 2	MENU 3	MENU 4	MENU 5
BREAKFAST	Mango Smoothie (see page 138) Porridge with Honey (see page 47)	Fresh orange juice Luxury Breakfast Muesli (see page 44)	Warm Prunes with Coconut and Orange Zest (see page 48) Slice of wholemeal toast with yeast spread Lemongrass Hot Drink (page 138)	Apple juice Coconut Pancake with Banana and Maple Syrup (see page 44)	Fresh orange juice Mini C's Fried Rice with Ham and Peas topped with Poached Egg (see page 49)
LUNCH	Carrot and Sweet Potato soup (see page 72) Chunky soda bread	Grilled Salmon Steaks with Creamy Lemon Sauce (see page 85) Green salad	Stuffed Peppers with Aromatic Rice (see page 96)	Shredded Omelette in Mild Broth (see page 75) Chunky wholemeal roll	Spicy Triple-flavour Noodle Soup with Broccoli and Beansprouts (see page 74)
EVENING MEAL	Baked Marinated Sea Bass with Mashed Sweet Potatoes (see page 85) Pear Crumble (see page 129)	Carrot and Pumpkin Risotto (see page 98) Spicy Chilled Cucumber and Ham Salad (see page 67)	Grilled Lamb Chops with Fresh Peppercorns, Coriander Roots and Shallots (see page 120) Grated carrot Green salad Watermelon Ice (see page 137)	Vegetable Lasagne (see page 106) Baked Apples with Walnuts and Custard (see page 129)	Chicken and Vegetables with Cashew Nuts and Roasted Dried Chillies (see page 116) Oriental Fruit Salad (see page 126)

It is best not to have a dessert every day though this is dependent on your weight and calorie requirements. One or two desserts per week is generally fine if you are looking to maintain your weight. On other days choose a favourite fruit instead.

Feeding the Children

Babies

If there is a history of severe food allergy in the family it is best for the mother to avoid that food when breastfeeding: in this case specialist advice should be sought. If children are going to develop a milk allergy, it usually happens in the first year of life and when cow's milk formula is introduced; they should grow out of it by three to five years of age. Lactose intolerance more often occurs later, in adult life. All mothers are encouraged to breastfeed exclusively for up to six months, if possible, and to start weaning from this time. Among other benefits this is thought to help prevent allergy, and can be particularly beneficial where there is a family history of allergies. It is a relatively new recommendation: the advice formerly given was to breastfeed exclusively until four months and start weaning then. In practice some babies appear to need weaning after four months. This is certainly something that should be discussed with your health visitor, registered dietitian or doctor, who can take your baby's individual health and medical details into account.

If your baby is diagnosed with cow's milk protein allergy, expert advice from a registered dietitian will be essential. Once the dairy-free diet commences, your child will return to being a happy healthy youngster. If you are not breastfeeding, you may be advised to feed your baby a hydrolysed milk formula (in which the cow's milk protein is broken down to its most basic form). In some cases a soya infant formula may also be recommended. Individual and specific advice will then be provided by your dietitian for following a dairy-free weaning process.

Young children

A healthy diet is essential for normal growth as well as physical and mental development. If healthy eating habits are formed young enough, these will be carried through to adult life. Taking a child off an important food group like dairy foods is safe as long as they are replaced with healthy alternatives like calcium-enriched soya drinks, yogurts and so on.

Once children get close to school age, they will notice if they have to do something different from their friends. Children do not like to be different from their peers, so it is important not to make an issue about any special dietary needs. Unfortunately many of the dairy foods that need to be avoided – such as puddings, ice cream, chocolate and custard – are favourites among children. This is why it is so important to provide enjoyable alternatives.

Breakfast

It sounds like a cliché but this is the most important meal of the day. Consistently going without breakfast places a child at significant risk of poor nutrition as their growing body will potentially be missing out on a third of its needs. A child who is poorly nourished will also be less alert, less able to concentrate at school and more tired overall. Invest in providing enough time to eat in the morning and to help encourage lifetime habits – try to make it fun. Breakfast can easily be boring if it is always the same. Buy in or prepare a variety of healthy cereals and baked foods like muffins and bagels, and stock up on a range of fresh calcium-enriched yogurt alternatives, drinks and favourite tinned fruit in natural juice. Puréed apple goes down a treat with young children; it can be made the night before, or a larger quantity can be prepared in advance and frozen in small amounts which can then be thawed as needed in the fridge overnight.

Breakfast suggestions

- Porridge with Honey (see page 47) and Mango Smoothie (see page 138)
- Warm Prunes with Coconut and Orange Zest (see page 48) with dairy-free muesli
- Mini C's Fried Rice with Ham and Peas topped with Poached Egg (page 49)

School dinners

Always make sure the school knows about any special dietary needs. If necessary, arrange a meeting with the caterer who will be able to advise on specific recipe ingredients and alternative options. Here are some suggestions for dairy-free school dinners:

- Jacket potato without butter, topped with tuna or baked beans
- Sweet-and-sour chicken with rice

- Roast chicken, potatoes and vegetables
- Spaghetti with meatballs
- Lamb casserole and potatoes
- Shepherd's pie (the mashed potato made with soya milk and vegan spread)

Dessert could be one of the following:

- Fruit
- Fruit jelly
- Fruit crumble
- Lemon meringue pie
- Flapjack
- Dairy-free custard

Lunch boxes

School dinners are not always an option and some children may prefer a lunch box. Aim to make the contents as varied as you can and pack in a rigid insulated cool box to ensure they are as fresh as possible. Try the following dairy-free suggestions:

- Pitta stuffed with chicken and salad, piece of fresh fruit, dairy-free calcium-enriched dessert, homemade flapjack or packet of raisins, dairy-free drink
- Chicken drumsticks, pitta bread, vegetable sticks, piece of fresh fruit, dairy-free yogurt (if this can be stored in a fridge until lunchtime), dairy-free muffin, dairy-free drink
- Salmon and vegetable wrap, piece of fresh fruit, homemade flapjack, dairy-free drink
- Couscous salad, piece of fresh fruit, dairy-free scone, orange juice
- Tuna, vegetable and rice salad, dried fruit, dairy-free dessert, carrot cake, dairy-free drink

It is important to go over the issues with your child's teacher but also to encourage children to manage their own allergies and intolerances and understand why swapping food with friends is not an option.

Afternoon tea and evening meal

Milky evening meals, which most children love, can all be made by directly substituting a dairy-free alternative for milk. These include many creamy pasta dishes, macaroni cheese, pancakes, lasagnes, custards and milky puddings. Many of these dishes can be made in bulk in advance and frozen. For plenty of inspiring evening-meal suggestions, look no further than the recipes in the second section of this book.

- Macaroni with Roast Cherry Tomatoes (see page 105)
- Carrot and Pumpkin Risotto (see page 98)
- Grilled Salmon Steaks with Creamy Lemon Sauce (see page 85)
- Fish Pie (see page 110)
- Pan-fried Chicken Breast with Creamy Basil Sauce (see page 88)

In addition, Mini C's Thai-style recipes bring lots of exciting new flavours and variety to the evening meal:

- Shredded Omelette in Mild Broth (see page 75)
- Steamed Cod Fillet with Triple-flavour Vegetables (see page 113)
- Steamed Chicken and Ginger Rice (see page 89)
- Yellow Curry with Lamb and Onions (see page 120)

Top tips for feeding babies and young children dairy-free

- Feed breast milk or the recommended infant formula for the first year.
- Weaning starts ideally at six months – but can start from four months. Suitable first foods include puréed potato, carrot, pear, apple (ripe banana and avocado not before six months).
- Avoid cow's milk until advised to reintroduce it by your health professional.
- Include foods rich in iron (e.g. red meat, egg yolk, green leafy vegetables, apricots, cereals) and vitamin C (e.g. citrus fruits, blackcurrants, kiwi fruit, green leafy vegetables, broccoli, green peppers and tomatoes) from six months.
- Avoid low-fat foods.
- Feed more varied meals by the end of the first year.
- By the age of one year a child should be eating three family-type meals per day, plus snacks such as toast, dairy-free calcium-enriched yogurt, fruit, vegetable sticks and fruit shakes – all according to individual appetite.
- Provide two to three servings of calcium-rich foods daily – see page 16.
- If children are away from home, make sure that their carers understand the dairy-free diet.

Eating Out

When you are following a completely dairy-free diet, you cannot leave eating out to chance. Advance planning goes a long way. Think carefully about restaurants, and meals which friends and family might serve. In no time, questioning and sometimes bringing along dairy-free foods and drinks will become second nature. Always tell your host about your requirements – it saves embarrassing and awkward moments on the day. Catering processes can often limit the number of safe choices on the menu if you are worried about contamination and depending on how strict your diet is. Phoning in advance and discussing the menu options with the restaurant manager or chef can really help and you can then relax and enjoy your evening more. The following tips will help you.

Chinese

Chinese cooking is one of the best options for dairy-free eating out. This type of cooking traditionally uses very little dairy. Good choices include: lemon chicken, vegetable chow mein, crispy duck, sweet-and-sour chicken and egg fried rice. Avoid the battered fruit and opt for fresh fruit such as the traditional lychees and sorbet.

Thai

Akin to Chinese, Thai food includes virtually no dairy products in its savoury dishes and very little in its desserts. Thai cooking tends to use coconut milk and cream in the same way as westerners use cow's milk and cream, so do be aware of the saturated fat content (see page 26 for more on this).

Mini C recommends the following options for eating out: glass noodle salad with minced pork and shrimps, green or red curry with beef and vegetables, stir-fried vegetables with garlic in mild broth, steamed or grilled sea bass with herbs, clear and mild cucumber soup with coriander and of course plain boiled rice. It is traditional to share such a meal, which allows you to control your intake. Watch out for desserts made with cow's milk and condensed or evaporated milk.

Italian

Italian food provides one of the more challenging but certainly not impossible choices for a dairy-free meal out. Most of the pizzas, pastas, risottos and lasagnes will be ruled out. Good choices include pasta with sun-dried tomato sauce (make sure butter is not used), focaccia and salads, or pizza with cheeseless toppings (choose your own at the restaurant). Alternatively some menus will provide a fresh fish and salad option. The breads on offer may be made with olive oil – ask the chef. Opt for fresh fruit desserts.

Indian

Traditionally ghee (clarified butter) is used for cooking Indian food. But in today's health-conscious environment vegetable ghee or oil tends to be substituted. Many dishes use yogurt and creamy dishes like korma will need to be avoided. Opt for vegetable curries made without yogurt and cream, rice and poppadams, and sorbet for dessert.

The pub

In the pub opt for the simple choices like grilled fish or lamb cutlets with baked potato. When requesting soup, ask for non-creamy options and always ask the manager or chef about the ingredients.

Burger bars

In burger bars, check that the bread is not made with butter or margarine and that the burger meat is not filled with any dairy source. Ask for a burger with a salad (check that the salad dressing is dairy-free) but no cheese. You can always bring your own dairy-free bun. Chicken pieces and drumsticks are an option if on offer. Many burger bars now have a comprehensive ingredients lists for their products which you may find on their website or alternatively ask the manager.

Going abroad

Order your dairy-free airline meal well in advance and find out what foods are available at your hotel and holiday destination. Consider taking some long-life dairy-free alternatives with you. It may also be worthwhile to learn how to ask for dairy-free options in the languages of the countries you are visiting or to have someone write this down on a piece of paper to show to the hotel or restaurant.

Commonly Asked Questions

Do I need to take calcium supplements if I am on a dairy-free diet?

If dairy is being swapped for a calcium-enriched dairy alternative, it is highly unlikely. However, it will depend on how much you have a day and the balance of intake in the rest of your diet. Those on a completely dairy-free regime should see a registered nutritionist to check the nutrient content of their diet.

I am following a low-GI diet: do the milk alternatives have a higher GI?

Very often the dairy equivalents are similar to dairy in terms of GI (glycaemic index) and also GL (glycaemic load) but it is important to check with individual manufacturers.

Do I need to check out drugs and medicines if I am on a dairy-free diet?

More than 20 per cent of prescription drugs and around 6 per cent of over-the-counter medicines contain lactose. Quantities are very small, so they should affect you only if you have a very severe allergy or lactose intolerance. However, to be on the safe side always check with your doctor or pharmacist before taking anything. If you do react to a medicine, it may be the medicine rather then the lactose that you have reacted to.

How soon after starting a dairy-free diet will I feel a difference?

This varies. If you have symptoms relating to either a lactose intolerance or an allergy, you can feel the difference within days to weeks of being on a dairy-free diet.

Further help and information

Following a restricted diet of any type can be tricky, sometimes isolating, especially when it's long-term. Hearing about experiences from others can be a great support. There is a number of organisations which offer further information and support – see pages 140–141 for details.

From the Chef

I found it very challenging to write the recipes for this book. Being Thai, I never really thought about dairy intolerances, simply because we hardly use dairy products in our cooking, if at all. So it was important for me find out more about lactose intolerance and how it affects people before I started writing the recipes.

When I researched the list of symptoms that can arise from consuming dairy products, one symptom really caught my eye and that was stomach pain. The description of the pain sounded so familiar and I suddenly thought to myself, perhaps I am actually one of those who suffers from this intolerance! I decided to test the theory by cutting out dairy products for two weeks just to see if my suspicion was right. To my great surprise, all the pain that I suffered totally vanished until I started adding milk to my tea and coffee and spreading butter on my toast again. I now use soya milk in my tea and cappuccino and substitute regular butter with vegan margarine whenever I can, although I do miss the real things from time to time. I have also learned a tremendous amount from Tanya Carr, our nutritionist and dietitian. She guided me on ingredients and held me on a tight rein, making sure that I kept everything within healthy eating guidelines!

The recipes in this book are half Thai and half western. The idea is that eastern food is generally a healthy way of eating dairy-free, and many of the Thai recipes included have been adapted for the purposes of a healthy dairy-free diet – for example some of them use soya milk. The western recipes provide dairy-free alternatives to dishes that traditionally contain cow's milk, such as ice cream, fish pie and clam chowder.

Although I am Thai and specialised in Thai cooking, I am quite familiar with cooking western dishes as I have spent a lot of time in the UK and US. But regardless of what you might think about Thai cooking, I can honestly tell you that western cooking is just as confusing if you don't have a basic idea of the ingredients used. I had one of our chefs, Wimuta, from the Busabong (my restaurant in London), as my assistant at the photoshoot. It was all going really well the first day when we did Thai dishes. However, when it came to making western dishes, he was totally shocked and found the whole process very frustrating. He could not believe there are so many steps involved in making one simple dish like a fish pie, and told me that he'd rather cook the 180 Thai dishes available on our menu on a daily basis than have to make *one* of these western recipes! But after a couple of days he became more familiar with the ingredients and from then on started to understand the process of western cooking.

Therefore, regardless of how well you think you can cook, it is vital to understand your ingredients before you can develop your creativity. Like me, you will find that using soya alternatives in recipes is surprisingly easy to do, and the results are delicious. We can all learn, be it fast or slow, and you will get there in the end… so let me guide you.

1 Breakfasts and Late-night Dishes

Luxury breakfast muesli

Bought muesli often contains dairy, but it is easy to make your own. You can prepare it in advance, but make sure you keep the toasted muesli and dried fruits separately in airtight containers in a cool, dry place. Just keep the soya milk within reach! **Serves 4**

- 50g (2oz) mixed nuts and seeds, such as almond flakes, chopped hazelnuts and sunflower seeds
- 125g (4½oz) unsweetened dairy-free muesli
- 100g (3½oz) mixed dried fruit, such as sun-dried small bananas, raisins, sultanas, dates, apricots and prunes, deseeded and chopped

To serve

- 1.2–1.8 litres (2–3 pints) soya milk
- Fresh peach and strawberry slices
- Brown sugar or runny honey (optional)

Toast the mixed nuts and seeds in a dry frying pan (do not use any oil) over a low heat until golden, tossing and turning them frequently to avoid burning. Remove from the heat and allow to cool; do not cover.

Toast the muesli in the same way and leave to cool.

Mix the dried fruit with the cooled nuts, seeds and muesli.

Serve the muesli with soya milk and, if you wish, some fresh peach and strawberry slices, and a sprinkling of brown sugar or drizzle of honey.

Per serving: 256 kcals, 9.1g fat, 1.3g saturated fat, 15.4g total protein, 8.8g soya protein, 360mg calcium, 0.05g sodium

Coconut pancake with banana and maple syrup

Being Thai, I find it difficult to get away from coconut whether that be coconut milk, juice or desiccated coconut. Coconut is one of the main ingredients in our cooking, so here it is – enjoy my kind of pancakes. **Serves 4**

- 3½ tablespoons caster sugar
- 4½ tablespoons rice flour
- 85g (3¼oz) plain flour, sifted
- 55g (2¼oz) desiccated coconut
- 1 large egg
- 300ml (½ pint) soya milk
- 3–4 dried figs, finely chopped
- 1 teaspoon grated lime zest
- A little vegan margarine or vegetable oil, for frying

For the maple syrup banana slices

- 1 tablespoon vegan margarine
- 2 bananas, peeled and cut into 5mm (¼in) rounds
- 2 tablespoons maple syrup
- 1½ tablespoons freshly squeezed lime juice

To serve

- Lime wedges
- Maple syrup

First make the maple syrup banana slices. In a frying pan, melt the margarine over a low heat and add the bananas. Gently stir until the slices are well coated. Add the maple syrup and lime juice and gently mix in. Remove from the heat and set aside.

Put the sugar, rice flour, plain flour and desiccated coconut in a large bowl and stir to mix well. In a separate bowl, beat the egg and soya milk together using a fork. Pour the egg mixture into the bowl of dry ingredients and gently incorporate, then whisk to form a batter, making sure there are no big lumps. Stir in the chopped figs and lime zest.

Heat a small amount of the margarine or oil in a non-stick frying pan. Pour in about 3 tablespoons of the mixture and quickly spread to a thin layer with the back of a spoon to keep an even thickness. Cook the pancake for about 40–50 seconds on a high heat until bubbles appear on the surface, then gently turn it over with a spatula and cook the other side until golden. Use the rest of the mixture to make more pancakes.

Serve the pancakes with the maple syrup, banana slices, lime wedges for squeezing and more maple syrup for drizzling.

Per serving: 489 kcals, 21.4g fat, 10.1g saturated fat, 8.7g total protein, 2.3g soya protein, 104mg calcium, 0.15g sodium

Warm sweet potatoes in ginger syrup

This is my most favourite sweet dish – it is very soothing. It is enjoyed by Thais as a snack at any time of day, and as it uses no dairy products I thoroughly recommend it to everyone on a dairy-free diet. **Serves 4**

600ml (1 pint) water
500g (18oz) sweet potatoes, peeled and cut into pieces about 2 x 1cm (¾ x ½in)
100g (3½oz) sugar
1 root of mature ginger, washed, cut into pieces and lightly pounded

Bring the water to the boil in a pan and put in the sweet potatoes. Once the water returns to the boil, add the ginger and continue to simmer for about 20 minutes until the potato pieces are tender and cooked through.
Add the sugar and stir gently until it is thoroughly dissolved.
Remove the pan from the heat and transfer the sweet potatoes into individual serving bowls, discarding the ginger pieces.

Per serving: 210 kcals, 0.4g fat, 0.2g saturated fat, 1.6g total protein, 33mg calcium, 0.05g sodium

Porridge with honey

Here is a healthy dairy-free and delicious way of making my favourite porridge. You can sweeten it to your own taste with a dash of runny honey or a sprinkling of brown sugar. It is also good with raisins. **Serves 4**

150g (5oz) porridge oats
700ml (1¼ pints) soya milk
700ml (1¼ pints) water
Runny honey or brown sugar (optional)
Raisins (optional)

Mix the oats, soya milk and water thoroughly in a sucepan.
Bring the mixture to the boil on a medium heat, then lower the heat and continue to simmer for approximately 5 minutes until the porridge thickens, stirring occasionally to prevent it sticking to the bottom of the pan.
Serve sweetened with honey or brown sugar and a sprinkling of raisins, if you wish.

Per serving: 187 kcals, 5.4g fat, 0.8g saturated fat, 10.5g total protein, 5g soya protein, 43mg calcium, 0.05g sodium

Warm prunes with coconut and orange zest

When we think of prunes, we think of a healthy breakfast or dessert, don't we? This dish makes a light but warm breakfast on a freezing morning. It is also a natural way to ease a constipation problem, if you have one! **Serves 4**

250g (9oz) stoned dried prunes
250ml (9fl oz) pure orange juice
1 large orange
2 tablespoons coconut cream
Soft brown sugar, for sprinkling

Place the prunes and orange juice in a pan and leave to soak for 30 minutes. Bring to the boil, then reduce the heat, cover and cook for approximately 20 minutes.

Meanwhile, thinly peel the zest (the orange-coloured part of the rind only) from the orange and cut it into fine shreds – you will need 2 tablespoons.

Spoon the cooked prunes into individual bowls, add ½ tablespoon of the coconut cream to each one and sprinkle with the orange zest and soft brown sugar to serve.

Per serving: 175 kcals, 2.6g fat, 2.2g saturated fat, 2.7g total protein, 55mg calcium, 0.01g sodium

Egg-fried bread drizzled with honey

The Thais call this 'French bread', though I still have no idea why. It is very popular among upper-class Thais and I must say it is yummy! It tastes and smells like a doughnut but with an alluring fragrance of honey. **Serves 4**

Vegetable oil, for deep-frying
4 medium eggs
4 medium slices of white bread
4 tablespoons runny honey

Heat enough oil to cover a slice of bread in a deep, wide frying pan over a medium heat until the temperature reaches about 180°C/356°F. If the oil is not hot enough before you add the bread, you will end up with very oily toasts.

Meanwhile, in a large bowl, beat the eggs with a fork until they have a runny texture.

Dip 1 slice of bread at a time into the eggs and coat it well, then gently place it in the frying pan, making sure it is covered with oil. Flip the bread over with tongs and continue to turn it backwards and forwards until it is golden brown. Deep-fry the remaining bread slices in the same way.

Remove the toasts from the pan with the tongs and drain them well on layers of folded kitchen paper.

Drizzle the toasts with honey and serve.

Per serving: 246 kcals, 11.3g fat, 2.2g saturated fat, 9.2g total protein, 68mg calcium, 0.25g sodium

Mini C's fried rice with ham and peas topped with poached egg

Typical Thai – rice for breakfast, lunch, dinner and even for a late-night snack. We can't get enough of it. The Thais treat rice in the same way as people in the west treat their bread and potatoes. **Serves 4**

- 400ml (14fl oz) vegetable or groundnut oil
- 310g (11oz) boneless skinless chicken, thinly sliced along the grain
- 310g (11oz) sliced cooked ham, cut into small square pieces
- 1kg (2¼lb) boiled rice (see right)
- 80g (3oz) onion, thinly sliced
- 80g (3oz) garden peas (shelled weight)
- 1 teaspoon sugar
- 2 teaspoons salt
- 2 tablespoons tomato ketchup
- 4 eggs

Heat a wok or frying pan over a medium heat, then add the oil and heat. Add the pieces of chicken and stir around until almost cooked, then add the ham and gently stir with the chicken for 30 seconds.

Add the boiled rice and toss and turn together with the ham and chicken pieces, then add the onion and peas. Stir the vegetables into the rice.

Season with the sugar, salt and tomato ketchup, stirring to make sure that the colour from the ketchup is evenly distributed.

Meanwhile, bring some water to the boil in a saucepan. Break the eggs, one by one, into a saucer and slip into the water. Turn off the heat and cover the pan. Leave to poach for 3 minutes until the whites are set but the yolks are still runny.

Serve the fried rice with the eggs on top.

Per serving: 619 kcals, 32.9g fat, 5.5g saturated fat, 38.5g total protein, 53mg calcium, 1.48g sodium

Boiled rice

Here are two ways of cooking rice: in a saucepan on top of a stove and using an electric rice cooker. In Thai cooking we do not season the rice with oil or salt. **Makes 1kg (2¼lb)**

- 400g (14oz) jasmine fragrant rice or plain long-grain rice
- 650ml (22fl oz) water

Using an electric rice cooker

Put the rice in a sieve and rinse it under warm running water until the water runs clear.

Place the rice in the pot that comes with the electric rice cooker and add the measured water.

Wipe all excess water from the outside of the pot, then place it back in the cooker and leave it to cook until the light switches off automatically.

Leave to stand for a further 10 minutes before serving the rice or using it in a recipe.

Using a pan

Rinse the rice well as described above, then put it in a saucepan with the measured water.

Place the pan over a medium-low heat and bring to the boil with the lid on. Stir the rice gently from time to time – take care not to break the grains. Once the water has begun to evaporate, turn the heat to very low and continue to simmer with the lid on.

When the water has completely evaporated and the rice is cooked, turn off the heat. Leave the pan to stand, covered, for a further 10 minutes before serving the rice or using it in a recipe.

Per serving: 330 kcals, 0.8g fat, 0.2g saturated fat, 7.7g total protein, 4mg calcium, 0.01g sodium

Rice soup with red snapper and coriander root

Coriander roots have an intense flavour and are widely used in Thai cooking. You can buy coriander with its roots still attached from Asian food stores. If unavailable, use the stalks of the herb instead. Serves 4

1.8 litres (3 pints) vegetable stock
3 fresh coriander roots, crushed
400g (14oz) boiled rice (see page 49)
2 tablespoons Thai fish sauce
2 teaspoons sugar
450g (1lb) red snapper fillets
Salt and ground white pepper

For the chillies in vinegar
4 large mixed chillies, sliced into thin rings
Distilled malt vinegar

For the crispy garlic
3 tablespoons vegetable oil
6 garlic cloves, crushed

To garnish
2 spring onions, chopped
Handful of coriander sprigs

First prepare the chillies in vinegar. Put the sliced chillies in a bowl and pour in enough vinegar to cover them completely. Leave to soak for a minimum of 30 minutes.

To make the crispy garlic, put the oil and crushed garlic in a frying pan or wok on a low heat and keep stirring until the garlic turns golden, but not burnt. Transfer into a bowl and set aside.

Pour the stock into a large pot, add the crushed coriander roots and bring to the boil. Add the cooked rice and simmer for 15 minutes. Season with the fish sauce and sugar, then add the fish fillets and simmer until the fish is cooked.

Transfer the rice soup into individual serving bowls, season with salt and pepper to taste and stir well. Garnish each bowl with the crispy garlic, spring onions and coriander springs, and serve with the chillies in vinegar on the side.

Per serving: 338 kcals, 10.3g fat, 1.3g saturated fat, 28.2g total protein, 118mg calcium, 1.34g sodium

2 Salads and Appetisers

Savoury assorted fruit salad with crispy shallots and rice crackers *This is a very summery dish and that's why it is popular in Thailand. It's an all-year-round dish for the Thais as our climate is almost always on the warm side.* Serves 2

½ handful of seedless grapes
1 Granny Smith apple, cored and chopped into small cubes
1 red apple, cored and chopped into small cubes
1 firm ripe papaya, peeled and chopped into small cubes
A few coriander leaves, to garnish
Rice crackers, to serve

For the dressing
1 tablespoon Thai fish sauce
1 bird's eye chilli, finely chopped
1 garlic clove, crushed
1 teaspoon caster sugar
25g (1oz) carrot, shredded
1½ tablespoons freshly squeezed lemon juice

For the crispy shallots
2 tablespoons vegetable oil
2 shallots, thinly sliced

First make the crispy shallots. Heat the oil in a wok over a medium heat. Add the shallot slices and deep-fry, stirring, until they turn golden brown and crisp. Remove from the hot oil and drain well on layers of kitchen paper. Leave to cool.

Make the dressing by combining the fish sauce, chilli, garlic and sugar in a bowl and stirring until the sugar dissolves. Add the carrot and lemon juice and mix well.

Put all the fruit in a large bowl, add the dressing and gently toss and turn. Add the crispy shallots and toss together one more time. Transfer to a large plate, sprinkle with coriander leaves and serve with rice crackers on the side.

Per serving: 249 kcals, 11.4g fat, 1.3g saturated fat, 2.8g total protein, 56mg calcium, 0.59g sodium

Cold wild rice salad with herbs *Rice is not usually eaten cold in Thailand, but I like it as long as it is served as a salad, such as this one. This recipe couldn't be simpler, it really is just a question of throwing ingredients together. Great for a packed lunch.* Serves 2

200g (7oz) hot cooked wild rice
Salt, to taste
1 tomato, chopped
3 tablespoons tinned kidney beans, drained and rinsed
2 tablespoons chopped red pepper
2 tablespoons chopped green pepper
1 tablespoon chopped basil leaves
1 garlic clove, crushed
1 teaspoon grated lime zest
1 tablespoon freshly squeezed lime juice
2 tablespoons freshly squeezed orange juice
Crispy shallots (see left)

Place the hot wild rice in a bowl and stir in salt to taste. Leave to cool.

Add all the remaining ingredients to the cooled rice and gently mix together well.

Per serving: 260 kcals, 11.7g fat, 1.4g saturated fat, 7.4g total protein, 39mg calcium, 0.19g sodium

Spinach and tomato quiche *This is the dish I make to entertain friends on a very casual day. It is one step up from a pizza, requiring slightly more preparation and effort, so your friends should feel a little more valued than if you were to serve them with a pizza!* Serves 6–8

- 225g (8oz) plain flour, plus extra for dusting
- 125g (4½oz) chilled vegan margarine, cut into small cubes
- Salt and ground black pepper
- 3½ tablespoons cold water
- 2 eggs and 2 egg yolks
- 450ml (16fl oz) soya cream
- 100g (3½oz) cheddar-style soya cheese, grated
- 1 courgette, thinly sliced
- 2 handfuls of spinach leaves, blanched, drained and excess water squeezed out
- 2 tomatoes, thinly sliced

Preheat the oven to 180°C/350°F/gas mark 6.

Place the flour, vegan margarine and half a teaspoon salt in a food processor and whizz until the mixture forms into crumbs. Add the water and whizz briefly again until a firm dough is formed. (You can also do this by hand.)

Roll out the dough on a floured worktop and use it to line a 22cm (8½in) loose-bottomed flan tin. Press the pastry well into the sides of the tin and trim away any excess hanging over the edge. Prick the bottom of the pastry case with a fork, then fill with crumpled foil.

Bake in the oven for 15 minutes or until the pastry is cooked through. Take the pastry case out of the oven and remove the crumpled foil. Lower the oven temperature to 160°C/325°F/gas mark 3.

Make the filling for the quiche by beating together the eggs and egg yolks and soya cream, until well blended. Stir in the grated cheese and all the prepared vegetables, then season with salt and pepper to taste.

Pour the filling into the pastry case and bake in the oven for 25–30 minutes until the filling is set and the surface is slightly brown.

Serve warm or cold with salad.

Per serving (for 8): 402 kcals, 30.1g fat, 5.6g saturated fat, 10.2 total protein, 2.2g soya protein, 190mg calcium, 0.35g sodium

Crispy vegetables with plum sauce

A healthier and dairy-free alternative to the usual battered foods. You can use any of your favourite vegetables, provided they are firm and solid in texture. For the plum sauce you can buy jars of salted plums in most Oriental supermarkets. **Serves 4**

240g (8½oz) plain flour
300ml (½ pint) water
½ teaspoon salt
1 teaspoon ground white pepper
Vegetable oil, for deep-frying
65g (2½oz) baby corn, trimmed
80g (3oz) broccoli florets, cut into bite-size pieces
80g (3oz) carrots, cut into sticks about 4cm (1½in) long and 1cm (½in) thick
80g (3oz) cauliflower florets, cut into bite-size pieces
80g (3oz) French beans, trimmed
1 large onion, cut into 8 sections

For the plum sauce

1 salted plum, stoned and mashed
175ml (6fl oz) distilled malt vinegar
100g (3½oz) sugar
125ml (4fl oz) water
1 tablespoon shredded carrot

First make the plum sauce. Place the salted plum, vinegar, sugar and water in a small saucepan over a low heat and stir until the sugar dissolves. Add the shredded carrot and simmer, stirring, until the sauce thickens. Remove from the heat and leave to cool. You can make this sauce weeks in advance, provided you keep it covered in the fridge, but be sure to return it to room temperature before using it so it isn't too sticky.

Put the flour in a large bowl, stir in the water and whisk to make a smooth paste. Add the salt and white pepper and give it a good whisk until the salt has dissolved.

Heat enough oil for deep-frying in a wok over a high heat until it reaches 180°C/356°F.

Dip each type of vegetable individually into the bowl of flour paste, then gently lift out a few pieces at a time and let the excess paste drip off.

Deep-fry the coated vegetables in batches in the hot oil until golden brown all over. Remove them from the wok using a wire spoon or tongs, drain them well on layers of kitchen paper and keep them warm. Repeat until all the vegetables are cooked.

Serve the crispy vegetables with the plum sauce on the side.

Per serving: 581 kcals, 26.5g fat, 3.1g saturated fat, 9.1g total protein, 135mg calcium, 0.46g sodium

Cashew nut salad with ginger and chillies

In Thailand, instead of having roasted peanuts with a cold beer in a pub, we tend to order more substantial snacks. This is a good example of how to convert plain cashew nuts into something more daring! **Serves 2–3**

- 150g (5½oz) raw cashew nuts
- 1 thumb-size piece of fresh root ginger, peeled and cut into matchsticks
- 2 bird's eye chillies, finely chopped
- 3 spring onions, sliced into thin rings
- A few grinds of sea salt

Preheat the oven to 160°C/325°F/gas mark 3 and dry-roast the cashew nuts for 5–10 minutes.

While the cashew nuts are still hot, place in a large bowl with the ginger, chillies and spring onions. Gently mix, then season with salt to taste and serve.

Per serving (for 3): 321 kcals, 27.5g fat, 3g saturated fat, 9.1g total protein, 20mg calcium, 0.21g sodium

Smoked salmon spicy salad

This is a lovely and fragrant salad which looks very colourful on the plate. It's a different way of serving smoked salmon – the dressing is quite refreshing with a bit of a kick from the chillies. Again, the ingredients are readily available. **Serves 2**

- 2 bird's eye chillies
- 2 garlic cloves
- 2 tablespoons lime juice
- 1 teaspoon caster sugar
- 200g (7oz) smoked salmon slices
- 4 shallots, thinly sliced
- 2.5cm (1in) piece of fresh root ginger, peeled and cut into matchsticks
- A few chives, cut into 5cm (2in) lengths, to garnish

Make a dressing by lightly crushing together the chillies and garlic cloves using a pestle and mortar. Add the lime juice and sugar and stir well to combine.

Put the smoked salmon in a large bowl, add the shallots and ginger, then pour over the dressing. Transfer to a large serving plate and garnish with chives.

Per serving: 166 kcals, 4.6g fat, 0.9g saturated fat, 26.4g total protein, 29mg calcium, 1.88g sodium

Grilled spiced scallops

This is my healthier version of Thai fast food, inspired by the charcoal-grilled fish, beef and pork balls on bamboo skewers sold on the streets all over Thailand. The sauce can be refrigerated for up to 3 months and used as a condiment as needed. Serves 4

2 garlic cloves, pounded with 1 fresh coriander root to make a paste
100ml (3½ fl oz) coconut cream
1½ tablespoons Thai fish sauce
½ teaspoon ground cumin
½ teaspoon ground coriander
½ teaspoon white pepper
500g (18oz) shelled scallops
2 large red peppers, deseeded, cut into 2.5cm (1in) squares
A few coriander leaves, to garnish

For the sweet chilli and garlic sauce

6 fresh red chillies
6 garlic cloves
175ml (6fl oz) distilled malt vinegar
110g (4oz) sugar
1 teaspoon salt

First make the sweet chilli and garlic sauce. Deseed 3 of the chillies and chop all 6 of them. Whizz the chillies and garlic in a small food processor, or pound them using a pestle and mortar, to form a paste. Heat the vinegar in a small pan over a low heat and stir in the sugar and salt until dissolved. Add the chilli and garlic paste and simmer, stirring occasionally, until the sauce thickens. Set aside to cool.

Combine the garlic and coriander paste with the coconut cream and fish sauce in a large bowl. Gently stir in the cumin, ground coriander and white pepper until well blended. Add the scallops to the paste, stirring to coat them, then cover and place in the fridge to marinate for about 20 minutes.

Soak 8–10 wooden skewers, 18cm (7in) long, in cold water.

Preheat the grill to high. Thread 3–4 scallops on to each skewer, alternating with pieces of red pepper. Grill the skewers for about 2 minutes, turning half-way through cooking, until the scallops are opaque.

Serve hot, drizzled with the sweet chilli and garlic sauce and garnished with coriander leaves.

Per serving: 351 kcals, 10.8g fat, 7.8g saturated fat, 27.2g total protein, 154mg calcium, 0.92g sodium

Aromatic seared tuna steak and citrus salsa

The Thais love to mix savoury ingredients with fruit. We even dip our fruit in spicy salt and sugar! This is a lovely, refreshing dish which is so light yet packed full of flavours. Serves 4

2 garlic cloves, finely chopped
1 teaspoon ground coriander
1 teaspoon salt
2 teaspoons freshly squeezed lime juice
4 tuna steaks
1 tablespoon olive oil
4 coriander sprigs, to garnish

For the citrus salsa

1 small orange or mandarin, peeled, membranes removed from each segment and cut into small pieces
½ grapefruit, prepared in the same way as the orange
Juice of 1 lemon
A few fresh pineapple slices, cut into small pieces
1 tomato, chopped
2 tablespoons chopped shallots
1 tablespoon Thai fish sauce
1 bird's eye chilli, crushed

Make a marinade by mixing the garlic, ground coriander, salt and lime juice in a large bowl. Add the tuna steaks one by one, turning them to make sure they are well coated with the mixture. Cover the bowl with clingfilm and leave to marinate in the fridge for about 30 minutes.

Prepare the citrus salsa while waiting for the fish to marinate. Mix all the salsa ingredients together well, cover and chill until needed.

Heat a griddle pan over a high heat and brush with the oil. Brush the tuna steaks on both sides with any remaining marinade and griddle for 2–3 minutes on each side.

Carefully cut each tuna steak into thin slices, garnish with the coriander sprigs and serve with the citrus salsa.

Per serving: 261 kcals, 9.8g fat, 2.7g saturated fat, 37.1g total protein, 52mg calcium, 0.85g sodium

Peanut-crusted black tiger prawns on shredded swede and carrot salad

I thought it would be interesting to have the crunchy texture of peanuts married closely with prawns, as they go so well together. See what you think. **Serves 4**

1 garlic clove, pounded with 1 fresh coriander root to make a paste
1½ tablespoons Thai fish sauce
75–90ml (3–3½fl oz) water
1 egg, beaten
80g (3oz) rice flour
25g (1oz) cornflour
2 kaffir lime leaves, finely shredded
½ teaspoon white pepper
Vegetable oil, for deep-frying
16 medium raw black tiger prawns, peeled and deveined but with the tails left on
80g (3oz) dry-roasted peanuts, coarsely chopped
4 coriander sprigs, to garnish

For the swede and carrot salad
1 teaspoon caster sugar
1 bird's eye chilli, crushed
1 tablespoon Thai fish sauce
1½ tablespoons freshly squeezed lemon juice
40g (1½oz) swede, cut into matchsticks
40g (1½oz) carrot, cut into matchsticks
1 large tomato, cut into wedges

Make the salad by mixing together the sugar, chilli, fish sauce and lemon juice in a bowl to make a dressing. Then add the swede, carrot and tomato and and gently toss and turn until they are all well coated in the dressing.

Mix the garlic and coriander paste with the fish sauce in a bowl. Whisk in 75ml (3fl oz) of the water and the beaten egg.

Combine the rice flour, cornflour, kaffir lime leaves and pepper in a separate bowl and slowly add the garlic and coriander mixture, and some more water if needed, to make a thick batter.

Heat enough oil for deep-frying in a wok over a high heat until it reaches 180°C/356°F. Holding each prawn by the tail, dip it in the batter, then coat it with the peanuts by using your other hand to sprinkle the peanuts all over it.

Slip the prawns carefully into the hot oil, 4 or 5 at a time, and fry until crisp and golden. Lift them out of the wok, drain them on layers of kitchen paper and keep them warm while you cook the remainder.

Arrange the swede and carrot salad on individual serving plates, place 4 of the crispy prawns on top of each portion, and garnish with a coriander sprig.

Per serving: 438 kcals, 27.4g fat, 4.1g saturated fat, 21.1g total protein, 95mg calcium, 1.03g sodium

Scented grilled fish salad

A very light and aromatic dish, full of flavour and fragrance. The coriander root and garlic paste really does make a difference to the taste of this monkfish salad and no doubt the dish would have been very bland without it! **Serves 2**

- 2 garlic cloves, pounded with 1 fresh coriander root to make a paste
- 100ml (3½fl oz) coconut cream
- 1 tablespoon Thai fish sauce
- ½ teaspoon ground cumin
- Ground black pepper
- 400g (14oz) monkfish fillet, cut into 12 cubes
- ½ red pepper, deseeded and cut into bite-sized pieces

To serve

- 2 tablespoons sweet chilli and garlic sauce (see page 60, or use ready-made)
- Mixed herb salad
- 1 lime

Combine the garlic and coriander paste with the coconut cream and fish sauce in a large bowl. Gently stir in the cumin and black pepper until well blended. Add the monkfish pieces, stirring to coat them, then cover and place in the fridge to marinate for about 20 minutes.

Soak 4 bamboo skewers, 18cm (7in) long, in cold water.

When you are ready to cook, preheat the grill to high. Thread 3 pieces of monkfish on to each skewer, alternating with pieces of red pepper. Grill for about 2 minutes, turning half-way through, until the fish is cooked.

Serve hot, drizzled with sweet chilli and garlic sauce on a bed of mixed herb salad with a squeeze of lime juice.

Per serving: 169 kcals, 9.3g fat, 7.6g saturated fat, 17.7g total protein, 22mg calcium, 0.31g sodium

Spicy smoked mackerel dip

At my restaurant we normally use a pestle and mortar to blend ingredients: this gives much greater control over the final texture. However, most households in the west are more likely to have a food processor, so that is what I have used here. **Serves 3–4**

- 6 garlic cloves
- 1 red onion, halved
- 110g (4oz) whole red and green chillies
- 110g (4oz) red and green peppers, deseeded
- 4 tablespoons Thai fish sauce
- ½ tablespoon sugar
- 4 tablespoons freshly squeezed lemon juice
- 2 tablespoons water, boiled and cooled
- 175g (6oz) smoked mackerel fillets, broken into small pieces
- Chopped coriander leaves, to taste
- Toasted bruschetta or fresh raw vegetables (such as carrots, celery, cucumber, tomatoes and courgettes), to serve

Preheat the oven to 150°C/300°F/gas mark 2.

Place the garlic, red onion, chillies and peppers on a baking tray and bake in the oven for about 45 minutes or until they are tender, turning once. Remove them from the oven and leave to cool a little.

Peel the skins off the chillies and peppers and cut the onion and peppers into small cubes.

Put the garlic and onion into the food processor first and gently blend to make a coarse paste. Add the chillies, peppers, fish sauce, sugar, lemon juice and water, followed by the fish pieces and blend to make a coarse paste.

Transfer the paste to a bowl and gently fold in the chopped coriander leaves to taste. This is great served with toasted bruschetta and also as a dip with fresh raw vegetables.

Per serving (for 3): 266 kcals, 18.5g fat, 4.5g saturated fat, 16.2g total protein, 51mg calcium, 1.98g sodium

Curried fishcakes *If you can't find grey feather fish paste in your local Oriental supermarkets and if cost is no object then use monkfish instead. The texture of the finished fishcakes must be quite bouncy so a fish like cod would not really be suitable.* **Makes 20 bite-size cakes (serves 4–5)**

1½ tablespoons vegetable oil, plus extra for deep frying
10 kaffir lime leaves, finely chopped
4 tablespoons ready-made Thai red curry paste
500g (18oz) pack grey feather fish paste, or monkfish fillet
1 egg
4 teaspoons sugar
2 tablespoons Thai fish sauce
Handful of green beans, trimmed and finely chopped
Handful of sweet basil leaves, chopped (optional)

For the chilli and peanut dip
225g (8oz) sweet chilli and garlic sauce (see page 60, or use ready-made)
25g (1oz) cucumber, quartered, deseeded and then finely chopped
25g (1oz) carrot, finely chopped
1½ tablespoons roasted peanuts, crushed
1 tablespoon distilled malt vinegar

First heat the measured oil in a wok or a saucepan and stir-fry half of the kaffir lime leaves with the red curry paste for about a minute, taking care not to burn the curry paste.
Make the chilli and peanut dip. Put all the ingredients in a bowl and stir together until blended, then set aside to cool.
To make the fishcakes, put the fish paste or monkfish, red curry paste, egg, sugar and fish sauce in a food processor and process until a thick paste forms, ensuring that the texture of the fish is chewy.
Transfer the paste to a large bowl and knead with your hands. Add the green beans, sweet basil leaves (if using) and the remaining kaffir lime leaves and continue to knead until all the ingredients are well distributed.
Lightly oil your fingertips, take 1 tablespoon of paste and roll it into a ball, then flatten it slightly by pressing. Continue in this way until all the mixture is used.
Heat enough oil for deep-frying in a wok over a high heat until it reaches 180°C/356°F.
Working in batches, fry the fishcakes, turning them often, until they are golden brown all over and float to the surface. Use a wire spoon to remove them from the hot oil, drain them well on kitchen paper and keep them warm. Continue until all the cakes are fried.
Serve the fishcakes with the chilli and peanut dip.

Per serving (for 4): 429 kcals, 23.1g fat, 2.9g saturated fat, 25.6g total protein, 64mg calcium, 0.24g sodium

Crispy prawn crêpes with cucumber relish

So fragile and delicious – please handle these with care once they are cooked. They taste like prawn crackers but with real prawns inside and feel very light, although they are deep-fried. The cucumber relish goes perfectly. **Serves 4**

400g (14oz) raw prawns, peeled and deveined
1 egg, beaten
1 tablespoon Thai fish sauce
Pinch of ground white pepper
1 garlic clove, pounded with ½ fresh coriander root to make a paste
8 large spring-roll wrappers, about 25cm (10in) square
Vegetable oil, for deep-frying

For the cucumber relish
225ml (8fl oz) distilled malt vinegar
125ml (4fl oz) water
3 tablespoons sugar
1 teaspoon salt
½ medium cucumber, quartered lengthways, deseeded and finely sliced
4 shallots, thinly sliced
2 fresh red chillies, finely sliced

First make the cucumber relish. Heat the vinegar and water in a small saucepan over a low heat. Add the sugar and salt and stir until dissolved. Remove from the heat and set aside to cool, then stir in the cucumbers, shallots and chillies.
Put the prawns into a food processor and whizz to make a thick paste. Transfer the paste to a bowl and stir in the beaten egg. Add the fish sauce, white pepper, and garlic and coriander paste and mix together with your hands, pressing and turning.
Divide the prawn paste between 4 of the spring-roll sheets, spreading it thinly over the whole surface. Top each one with another sheet and use a rolling pin to seal the sheets together.
Cut each large prawn crêpe into 4 equal square pieces, making a total of 16 smaller crêpes, sealing each one as before.
Heat enough oil for deep-frying in a pan over a high heat to about 180°C/356°F. Lower a few crêpes at a time gently into the oil and keep turning them until golden brown all over. Use a pair of tongs or a wire spoon to remove them from the wok and drain on kitchen paper. Keep warm while you fry the rest.
Serve with the cucumber relish.

Per serving: 505 kcals, 23g fat, 2.9g saturated fat, 26.8g total protein, 134mg calcium, 1.36g sodium

Caesar salad with chicken

If Caesar salad is your favourite then why not try this dairy-free version – I guarantee you will be pleasantly surprised. Please note that children, pregnant women and the elderly should not eat undercooked eggs. **Serves 4**

2 tablespoons olive oil
4 thick slices of day-old bread, cut into 1cm (½in) cubes
1 Cos lettuce
25g (1oz) vegan Parmesan-style cheese, finely pared into shavings, or grated

For the dressing
5 tablespoons olive oil
4 garlic cloves
2 tinned anchovy fillets in oil, drained and chopped
1 tablespoon balsamic vinegar
5 teaspoons Dijon mustard
1 egg

For the chicken
1 tablespoon olive oil
Sea salt and black pepper
2 skinless boneless chicken breasts

Preheat the oven to 220°C/425°F/gas mark 7.
Put the oil in a bowl, add the bread cubes and toss to coat in the oil. Place the bread cubes on a baking sheet and bake in the oven for 6 minutes or until crisp and golden. Set aside.
Reduce the oven temperature to 180°C/350°F/gas mark 4 to cook the chicken. Mix the olive oil with salt and pepper to taste and rub all over the chicken. Cook in the oven for about 20 minutes or until cooked through. Slice and keep warm.
Meanwhile, make the dressing. Put the oil in a small saucepan, add the whole garlic cloves and the anchovies and heat gently for 5 minutes until the garlic is soft and golden. Allow to cool, then strain the oil and reserve. Mash the garlic and anchovies to a paste and mix in the vinegar and mustard. Gradually whisk in the strained oil in a steady stream until the mixture thickens.
Cook the egg in boiling water for only 2 minutes, then cool it under cold running water. Shell the egg and whisk only the yolk directly into the dressing until evenly combined.
Tear the lettuce leaves into a large salad bowl. Scatter over the croûtons and cheese shavings, pour on the dressing and toss well. Arrange the warm sliced chicken on top and serve.

Per serving: 455 kcals, 28.3g fat, 5.2g saturated fat, 26.6g total protein, 151mg calcium, 0.68g sodium

Thai grilled beef salad

This is very Thai. It is another way of making beef more interesting, apart from the usual stir-frying and stewing methods. Although quite a filling dish, it is great for your waistline as long as you trim any fat from the beef. Especially great with an ice-cold beer! **Serves 2**

- Vegetable oil or butter, for greasing
- 400g (14oz) beef topside, in one piece
- 2 bird's eye chillies
- 2 garlic cloves, roughly chopped
- 3 tablespoons Thai fish sauce
- 4½ tablespoons freshly squeezed lemon juice
- ½ tablespoon caster sugar
- 80g (3oz) cucumber, finely sliced
- 2 tomatoes, cut into wedges
- ½ onion, thinly sliced
- 2 spring onions, chopped
- ½ handful of coriander leaves, to garnish

Preheat the grill to medium-high and lightly grease the grill rack.

Place the beef on the rack and grill for 2–3 minutes on each side until it is medium-rare, then set aside to cool.

Pound the chillies and garlic together into a paste using a pestle and mortar. Transfer to a large bowl and stir in the fish sauce, lemon juice and sugar.

Thinly slice the beef and add it to the bowl, along with the cucumber, tomatoes, onion and spring onions and very gently toss together.

Transfer the salad to serving bowls and garnish with the coriander leaves.

Per serving: 375 kcals, 16g fat, 6.9g saturated fat, 45.7g total protein, 54mg calcium, 1.83g sodium

Spicy chilled cucumber and ham salad

This salad, with an oil-free dressing, is so simple to make and the ingredients are pretty common and easily found, especially in your own fridge! It's important to use good-quality ham. **Serves 2**

- 200g (7oz) cooked sliced ham, cut into long thin strips
- 1 large cucumber, halved lengthways, deseeded and sliced
- ½ onion, thinly sliced into rings
- A few coriander sprigs, to garnish

For the dressing

- 2 garlic cloves, crushed
- 2 bird's eye chillies, lightly crushed
- ½ tablespoon caster sugar
- 4 tablespoons Thai fish sauce
- 6 tablespoons freshly squeezed lemon juice

Make the dressing by combining the garlic, chillies, sugar, fish sauce and lemon juice in a bowl. Mix well and set aside.

Place the ham, cucumber slices and onion rings in a large bowl, then pour the dressing over. Gently stir and toss to make sure the dressing is well absorbed into the salad ingredients.

Transfer to a serving bowl and garnish with the coriander.

Per serving: 209 kcals, 5.3g fat, 1.9g saturated fat, 27.6g total protein, 76mg calcium, 3.37g sodium

Crispy roast duck salad with shredded carrots and cabbage

Last summer I added a few new dishes to the menu at the Busabong, my restaurant in Chelsea, that would be suitable for the hot weather. This dish was one of them. Serves 2

225g (8oz) roasted boneless skinless duck breast, thinly sliced
Plain flour, for coating
Vegetable oil, for deep-frying
250g (9oz) white cabbage, cored and thinly sliced
80g (3oz) carrots, cut into matchsticks
2 garlic cloves, crushed
2 bird's eye chillies, lightly crushed
½ tablespoon caster sugar
4 tablespoons Thai fish sauce
6 tablespoons freshly squeezed lemon juice
A few coriander sprigs, to garnish

Sprinkle the duck slices with a little water, then coat them with the flour, shaking off any excess.
Heat enough oil for deep-frying in a wok over a high heat until it reaches 180°C/356°F.
Add the duck slices and deep-fry for about 1–2 minutes, stirring them around, until they become golden brown and crisp. Use a wire spoon to remove the duck slices from the oil and drain them well on kitchen paper.
Mix the cabbage and carrots together in a bowl, then add the garlic, chillies, sugar, fish sauce and lemon juice and toss together again until well combined.
Transfer the salad to a serving bowl and scatter the crispy duck on top, then garnish with the coriander sprigs.

Per serving: 557 kcals, 36g fat, 5.8g saturated fat, 33.1g total protein, 33mg calcium, 2.43g sodium

Fragrant minced pork on lemongrass stalks

Pork is quite affordable and can be very tasty if prepared well with the right ingredients. The 'skewers' for this recipe are lemongrass stalks, which lend extra flavour and aroma to the finished dish. Serves 4

400g (14oz) minced pork
2 tablespoons coconut cream
2 teaspoons ready-made Thai red curry paste
1 egg yolk
2 teaspoons shredded kaffir lime leaves
12 lemongrass stalks
½ handful of basil leaves, to garnish
Lemon and lime zest, to garnish
Sweet chilli and garlic sauce (see page 60, or use ready-made), to serve

Preheat the grill or heat the barbecue.
Mix together the minced pork, coconut cream, red curry paste, egg yolk and kaffir lime leaves in a bowl. Using your hands, gently pack an equal amount of the mixture on to each of the lemongrass stalks.
Grill or barbecue the minced pork on lemongrass stalks for 10–15 minutes until cooked, turning occasionally.
Serve garnished with the basil leaves and lemon and lime zest and accompanied by the sweet chilli and garlic sauce.

Per serving: 218 kcals, 14.6g fat, 6.3g saturated fat, 20.7g total protein, 29mg calcium, 0.1g sodium

3 Soups and One-plate Meals

Carrot and sweet potato soup

The colour of this soup is incredible – when I see it I feel like diving into the soup bowl! Both the colour and texture are so inviting and, of course, the taste is unmistakable for its natural sweetness. **Serves 2**

- 10g (½oz) vegan margarine or 1 tablespoon extra virgin olive oil
- ½ onion, chopped
- 2 large carrots, chopped
- 1 medium sweet potato, peeled and chopped
- 600ml (1 pint) vegetable stock
- 50ml (2fl oz) soya cream
- Salt and pepper
- 1 tablespoon chopped coriander leaves

Heat the margarine or olive oil in a saucepan over a medium heat. Stir in the onion, carrots and sweet potato and cook for about 4 minutes.

Add the vegetable stock, bring to the boil and simmer for 25 minutes until the carrots and sweet potatoes are soft. Remove from the heat and leave to cool slightly.

Purée the soup in a blender until smooth and creamy. Return it to the pan, stir in the soya cream and reheat. Season with salt and pepper to taste, add the coriander and serve hot.

Per serving: 198 kcals, 9.3g fat, 1.6g saturated fat, 4.1g total protein, 120mg calcium, 0.59g sodium

Green pea soup

This is one soup that I never serve with any bread. I like its richness. It's a good idea to reserve a few whole peas to add to the soup just before serving to give it extra texture. The crispy bacon provides another dimension: it is fairly salty, so be careful how much salt you add to the soup. **Serves 2**

- 10g (½oz) vegan margarine
- ½ white onion, chopped
- 500g (18oz) vegetable stock
- 500g (18oz) fresh green peas
- 50ml (2fl oz) soya milk
- Salt and pepper
- 1 tablespoon chopped parsley
- 2 tablespoons soya cream (optional)
- 3 rashers of smoked streaky bacon, cut into small pieces and fried until crisp

Melt the margarine in a large saucepan and stir in the onion. Cook until it is light golden, add the stock and bring to the boil. Add the peas, return to the boil and simmer for a few minutes or until the peas are tender and soft. Remove from the heat.

Add the soya milk, allow to cool slightly, then purée the soup in a blender until smooth and creamy.

Return the soup to the pan and gently reheat. Season to taste and stir in the parsley. Pour into individual serving bowls, top each with 1 tablespoon of soya cream, twirled in the centre (if using), and sprinkle with crispy bacon.

Per serving: 342 kcals, 12.7g fat, 4.1g saturated fat, 27.6g total protein, 0.8g soya protein, 105mg calcium, 1.08g sodium

Spicy triple-flavour noodle soup with broccoli and beansprouts

I call this triple-flavour soup because it really does live up to its name. It is healthy and easy to prepare. Once you have tried it, you will be hooked! **Serves 2**

- 150g (5oz) dried wide rice noodles, soaked in cold water for an hour and drained
- 125g (4½oz) beansprouts
- 850ml (1½ pints) vegetable stock
- 2 garlic cloves, lightly pounded
- 2 fresh coriander roots, lightly pounded
- 80g (3oz) broccoli florets, cut into bite-size pieces
- 4 tablespoons Thai fish sauce
- 2 tablespoons sugar
- 2 tablespoons distilled malt vinegar
- 2 tablespoons crushed peanuts
- 1 fresh red chilli, sliced into fine rounds
- 3 tablespoons freshly squeezed lemon juice
- ½ teaspoon chilli powder (optional)
- Coriander leaves, to garnish

Bring a saucepan of water to the boil over a high heat. Add the noodles and continue boiling for about 1 minute until the noodles are soft, then immediately add the beansprouts. Leave for about 15 seconds, then drain well. Transfer the noodles and beansprouts to 2 individual serving bowls and set aside.

Bring the stock to the boil in the same saucepan and add the pounded garlic, coriander roots and broccoli. Reduce the heat and simmer for about 2 minutes until the garlic and coriander roots release their aroma. Season the soup with the fish sauce, sugar, vinegar, peanuts and chilli rings.

Divide the soup equally between the bowls, immediately adding the lemon juice and chilli powder (if using) to each serving. Garnish with the coriander leaves and serve.

Per serving: 465 kcals, 7.9g fat, 1.4g saturated fat, 17.7g total protein, 137mg calcium, 2.88g sodium

Pumpkin and basil soup

The Thais use a lot of pumpkin in their cooking which is why I was inspired to create this healthy and tasty soup. Pumpkins from different parts of the world vary hugely in texture (those from Thailand can be quite hard) and cooking times differ accordingly. **Serves 2**

- 1 litre (1¾ pints) water
- 400g (14oz) pumpkin (peeled and deseeded weight), cut into chunks
- 2 potatoes, peeled and diced
- Salt and pepper
- 65ml (2½fl oz) extra virgin olive oil
- 1 garlic clove, finely sliced
- 2 shallots, finely chopped
- 6 basil leaves, chopped

Bring the water to the boil in a large pan. Add the pumpkin and potato pieces and cook on a low heat until tender.

Mash the pumpkin and potato with a fork to thicken the soup and keep simmering. Season to taste with salt and pepper.

Meanwhile, in another saucepan, heat the oil, add the garlic and shallots and stir-fry until the garlic is golden. Pour the garlic, shallots and oil into the soup, add the basil, stir well and serve.

Per serving: 390 kcals, 30.2g fat, 4.2g saturated fat, 4.4g total protein, 71mg calcium, 0.1g sodium

Shredded omelette in mild broth *In Thailand this is called poor man's soup. I'll tell you, though, that if a poor man's food tastes this good, I'll swap places with him for a while! It's mild and gentle, yet full of flavour. Really delicious!*

Serves 2

600ml (1 pint) vegetable stock or water
1 fresh coriander root, lightly pounded
175g (6oz) cucumber, halved, deseeded and roughly chopped
40g (1½oz) onion, coarsely chopped
2 tablespoons Thai fish sauce
1½ teaspoons sugar
2 spring onions, cut into 2.5cm (1in) lengths
2 tablespoons coriander leaves
Pinch of ground black pepper

For the shredded omelette

1 tablespoon vegetable oil
1 egg, beaten

For the crispy garlic

1 tablespoon vegetable oil
2 garlic cloves, finely crushed

To make the shredded omelette for the garnish, heat the oil in a frying pan over a medium-high heat and swirl the oil to cover the whole surface of the pan. Pour in the egg and swirl it around the pan to form a thin layer. Cook until the omelette is set, then tip it out of the pan. Roll up the omelette into a tight cylinder, and cut it across into thin strips. Set aside.

To make the crispy garlic, heat the oil, add the garlic and fry over a low heat until it is golden and crisp. Drain well on kitchen paper and set aside.

Place the stock or water in a saucepan over a high heat and bring to the boil. Add the coriander root, reduce the heat to low and simmer for 10 minutes. Increase the heat to medium and add the cucumber and onion. Season with the fish sauce and sugar, stir well and leave to simmer for another 3 minutes.

Add the spring onions, then transfer the soup to individual serving bowls. Scatter the shredded omelette on top, sprinkle with the crispy garlic, coriander leaves and pepper, then serve.

Per serving: 88 kcals, 7g fat, 1g saturated fat, 3g total protein, 37mg calcium, 0.32g sodium

Clam chowder *I had not realised how difficult it could be to get a tin of clams – it is quite easy to get fresh ones when they are in season. If you can't find either tinned or fresh, just go for cockles: this will still result in a very good chowder.*

Serves 2

- ½ tablespoon vegetable oil
- ½ leek, chopped
- ½ onion, chopped
- 2 medium potatoes, peeled and cubed
- 150ml (¼ pint) vegetable stock
- 150g (5oz) tin of clams in brine, drained
- 1 teaspoon arrowroot
- 200ml (7fl oz) soya milk
- Salt and pepper
- 2 coriander sprigs

Heat the oil in a large saucepan, add the leek and onion and cook for a few minutes until soft. Add the potatoes and cook for a further 3 minutes, stirring frequently.

Pour in the stock and leave to simmer for about 25 minutes until the vegetables are soft.

Add the clams and arrowroot and simmer and stir for a further 5 minutes until the clams are heated through and the chowder has thickened.

Stir in the soya milk and reheat gently. Season with salt and pepper, pour into individual serving bowls and garnish each one with a coriander sprig.

Per serving: 258 kcals, 5.5g fat, 0.7g saturated fat, 23.7g total protein, 3g soya protein, 127mg calcium, 1.54g sodium

Pasta and chickpea soup *I don't often use chickpeas in my cooking because of the overnight-soaking bit. But you could say to me that sticky rice needs the same soaking time and you are absolutely right. I suppose it's all about forward planning!* Serves 2

- 125g (4½oz) dried chickpeas, soaked overnight and drained
- 2 tablespoons chopped rosemary
- 3 garlic cloves, chopped
- 3 tablespoons extra virgin olive oil
- 600ml (1 pint) water
- 150g (5oz) penne pasta
- Salt and pepper

Combine the chickpeas, rosemary, garlic, half the olive oil and the water in a saucepan. Bring to the boil, lower the heat and simmer for about 1½ hours or until the chickpeas are soft.

Remove from the heat and allow to cool a little. Transfer the chickpeas to a food processor and whizz to a purée. Return it to the pan and gently reheat.

Meanwhile, bring a large pan of salted water to the boil. Add the pasta and cook until it is *al dente,* then drain.

Add the cooked pasta to the hot chickpea soup, season to taste and serve.

Per serving: 622 kcals, 21.5g fat, 3.9g saturated fat, 23g total protein, 140mg calcium, 0.13g sodium

Plantain and herb soup with chicken

Plantains resemble large bananas. They usually look bruised and battered, but inside, once the skin is peeled off, they have amazing blushed-pink flesh that is delicious when cooked. **Serves 2**

700ml (1¼ pints) water
2 fresh coriander roots, lightly pounded
4 kaffir lime leaves, torn
2 lemongrass stalks, lightly pounded
2cm (¾in) piece of galangal, finely sliced into very thin rounds
4½ tablespoons Thai fish sauce
2 teaspoons sugar
310g (11oz) boneless chicken breast, thinly sliced
1 plantain, peeled and sliced into rounds about 5mm (¼in) thick
4 plum tomatoes, quartered
1 onion, quartered
2 large dried chillies, deep-fried in hot oil for 1 minute, drained and each cut across into 4 pieces
4 tablespoons freshly squeezed lemon juice
Coriander leaves, to garnish

Bring the water to the boil in a saucepan over a high heat. Reduce the heat to low, add the coriander roots, kaffir lime leaves, lemongrass and galangal and simmer for about 10 minutes, until the herbs have released their aroma.

Stir in the fish sauce and sugar, then add the chicken, plantain, tomatoes and onion. Turn up the heat and continue simmering until the chicken is well cooked. Turn off the heat and add the chillies and lemon juice.

Transfer the soup into individual serving bowls and garnish with the coriander leaves.

Per serving: 394 kcals, 4.3g fat, 0.9g saturated fat, 45.1g total protein, 82mg calcium, 2.72g sodium

Chicken soup with straw mushrooms and toasted sesame seeds

This is a very simple, light and soothing soup. If you would like to turn it into a more substantial dish, all you have to do is to add some boiled rice or egg noodles. **Serves 2**

850ml (1½ pints) chicken stock
150g (5oz) boneless chicken breast, thinly sliced
2 tablespoons light soy sauce
Salt, to taste
1 teaspoon black peppercorns
2 thumb-size pieces of fresh root ginger, lightly crushed
6 chestnut mushrooms, washed and trimmed
6 dried straw mushrooms, soaked in warm water until soft, drained, squeezed dry and sliced into thin strips
1 spring onion, finely sliced into rounds
1 teaspoon sesame seeds, dry-fried on a low heat until golden brown
2 tablespoons coriander leaves

Bring the chicken stock to the boil in a saucepan, and add the soy sauce, salt to taste, peppercorns and ginger, cover with a lid and leave to simmer for about 5 minutes.

Add the chicken slices and simmer for 2 minutes. Then add both types of mushrooms and simmer for a couple more minutes until the chicken is cooked but still tender.

Transfer the soup into individual serving bowls, discarding the ginger and sprinkle with the spring onion, toasted sesame seeds and coriander leaves.

Per serving: 146 kcals, 2.9g fat, 0.5g saturated fat, 23.1g total protein, 111mg calcium, 1.76g sodium

Asparagus soufflé

The asparagus gives this soufflé a really vibrant colour. If you've never tried making a soufflé before, then try this recipe – it is a real gem. If you prefer a non-vegetarian version, just add about 65g (2½oz) crabmeat to the mixture. **Serves 2**

12 asparagus spears
200ml (7fl oz) soya milk
½ onion, thinly sliced
20g (¾oz) spring onion, finely chopped
½ red pepper, sliced into strips
25g (1oz) vegan margarine, plus extra for greasing
2 tablespoons plain flour
Salt and ground white pepper
4 eggs, separated, and 1 egg white

Cut 4 of the asparagus tips into 3 pieces each, blanch for 1 minute and set aside. Boil the remaining asparagus in water for a few minutes until tender, drain well and leave to cool. Process the boiled asparagus in a blender until smooth, then rub through a fine sieve to make a purée. Set aside.

Put the soya milk in a saucepan with the onion, spring onion, red pepper and blanched asparagus. Bring slowly to the boil, remove from the heat, cover and leave to infuse for 30 minutes. Strain the soya milk from the vegetables and set both aside.

Preheat the oven to 180°C/350°F/gas mark 4. Grease a 1.3-litre (2¼-pint) soufflé dish.

Melt the margarine in a pan, stir in the flour and cook gently for a minute, stirring. Remove the saucepan from the heat and stir in the strained soya milk. Bring slowly to the boil and continue to cook, stirring, until the sauce thickens. Stir in the asparagus purée, season to taste and set aside to cool slightly. Beat the egg yolks into the cooled sauce one at a time.

Whisk the egg whites until they stand in soft peaks. Mix 1 large spoonful of egg white into the sauce to lighten its texture, pour the sauce over the remaining egg whites and gently fold in. Pour the mixture into the prepared dish, smooth the surface with a palette knife and scatter the cooked vegetables on top.

Place the soufflé dish on a baking sheet and bake for 30 minutes until the soufflé is golden brown, well risen and just firm to the touch. Serve hot.

Per serving: 431 kcals, 27.8g fat, 6.3g saturated fat, 25.9g total protein, 3g soya protein, 160mg calcium, 0.45g sodium

Pad Thai with coconut milk

Pad Thai is Thailand's most famous and popular fried noodle dish. It is not generally made with coconut milk, but this adds extra flavour, so do try it. If you think that you still prefer the usual recipe, simply omit the coconut milk next time you make it. **Serves 2**

1 tablespoon vegetable oil
6 raw black tiger prawns, peeled, deveined and de-headed; tails left on
25g (1oz) cooked shrimps
1 egg
100g (3½oz) dried rice noodles, soaked in cold water for 1 hour and drained
1½ tablespoons Thai fish sauce
1½ tablespoons distilled malt vinegar
4 tablespoons coconut milk
2 spring onions, cut into 2.5cm (1in) lengths
1 small carrot, cut into matchsticks
80g (3oz) beansprouts
1½ tablespoons crushed roasted peanuts
1 tablespoon crushed pickled turnip (*hoa chai-pho*), optional
1½ tablespoons sugar
2 lime wedges, to serve
Chilli powder (optional)
Coriander leaves, to garnish

Heat a wok over a high heat. Add the oil, turn the heat to medium, add the prawns and stir-fry for about 30 seconds until they are half-cooked. Add the shrimps, crack in the egg and keep turning until the egg is well done and looks like uneven, broken pieces of a cooked omelette.

Immediately stir in the noodles, season with the fish sauce and vinegar and continue stir-frying, constantly tossing and turning the ingredients, but taking care not to break the noodles. Add the coconut milk and stir well, using the corner of a spatula so the noodles don't break.

Add the spring onions, most of the carrot and most of the beansprouts, some of the peanuts, the turnip and sugar, stirring until all the ingredients are well blended.

Divide the noodles between 2 plates. Garnish with the reserved carrot, beansprouts, peanuts and lime wedges. Sprinkle with a little chilli powder (if using) and coriander leaves and serve.

Per serving: 477 kcals, 18.8g fat, 6.6g saturated fat, 21.3g total protein, 135mg calcium, 1.51g sodium

Baked pineapple rice and roasted pine nuts

This is supposed to be a Thai-style savoury rice. However, adding ingredients such as pine nuts and raisins makes it a little more western. Most of all, it's the baking method that really makes this rice cosmopolitan. **Serves 2**

1 large pineapple
1 tablespoon pine nuts
2 tablespoons vegetable oil
1 tablespoon frozen peas
2 tablespoons diced carrot
1 tablespoon raisins
2 eggs
400g (14oz) steamed rice
Salt, to taste
1½ tablespoons light soy sauce
Ground white pepper
1 chopped red chilli, to garnish

Preheat the oven to 150°C/300°F/gas mark 2.

Cut the pineapple in half lengthways and scoop out the flesh. Chop half the flesh into small chunks and reserve for use in this recipe; the remaining flesh can be used in another dish – perhaps a refreshing dessert.

Dry-fry the pine nuts in a frying pan until golden brown, then remove from the pan and set aside. Heat the oil in the same pan and stir-fry the pineapple chunks, peas, carrot, raisins and pine nuts. Add the eggs, breaking the yolks, and continue to stir-fry with the rest of ingredients until well cooked.

Stir in the rice, mix well with the other ingredients, season with salt to taste and the light soy sauce and remove from the heat. Divide the rice equally between the pineapple shells, cover with foil and bake in the oven for 10–15 minutes.

Serve sprinkled with ground white pepper and garnished with the chilli slices.

Per serving: 606 kcals, 24.1g fat, 3.7g saturated fat, 15.1g total protein, 91mg calcium, 1g sodium

Thai savoury rice porridge with tiger prawns and crispy garlic

Most Thai people would have this soup for breakfast when on holiday in summer at their beach houses by the sea. It's usually made with minced pork, but this prawn version is equally good. **Serves 2**

- 850ml (1½ pints) chicken stock
- 2 fresh coriander roots, lightly pounded
- 200g (7oz) boiled rice (see page 49)
- 225g (8oz) black tiger prawns, peeled and deveined, tails left on
- 1 teaspoon sugar
- 2 tablespoons Thai fish sauce
- 2 eggs
- 1 thumb-size piece of fresh root ginger, peeled and cut into matchsticks
- Crispy garlic (see page 75)
- 1 spring onion, chopped
- ½ teaspoon ground white pepper
- Coriander leaves, to garnish

Put the chicken stock in a saucepan, add the pounded coriander roots and bring to the boil, then discard the coriander roots and add the cooked rice. Remove from the heat and leave to cool slightly.

Transfer to a food processor and blend until the grains have broken up to form a paste. Pour back into the saucepan and bring to the boil. Add the prawns and season with the sugar and fish sauce. Cook over a high heat for about 2 minutes. (Water can be added if you like the soup quite watery, but in this case remember to increase the amount of seasoning.)

Pour the soup into individual serving bowls. Crack an egg into each bowl and stir so that the egg cooks in the hot soup. Scatter with the ginger matchsticks and crispy garlic.

Sprinkle with the spring onion, ground white pepper and coriander leaves.

Per serving: 391 kcals, 13.5g fat, 2.5g saturated fat, 34.2g total protein, 201mg calcium, 2g sodium

Seafood and glass noodle casserole

This is a very gingery and aromatic dish. I always find that sesame oil and ginger go very well together. If you can't get hold of fermented soya beans, use 2 tablespoons of light soy sauce.

Serves 2

- 150g (5oz) dried glass noodles, soaked in water for 10 minutes and drained
- 6 dried straw mushrooms, soaked in warm water until soft, squeezed dry and sliced into thin strips
- 2 fresh coriander roots, lightly pounded
- 2 garlic cloves, lightly pounded
- ½ thumb-size piece of fresh root ginger, peeled and cut into matchsticks
- 1 tablespoon light soy sauce
- 1 tablespoon fermented soya beans
- 2 tablespoons sesame oil
- 300ml (½ pint) chicken stock
- 6 crab claws
- 6 medium headless raw prawns, peeled and deveined
- 1 spring onion, chopped
- ½ teaspoon ground white pepper
- 2 tablespoons chopped coriander, including the stems
- Sweet chilli and garlic sauce, to serve (optional), see page 60, or use ready-made

Mix the noodles with the mushrooms, coriander roots, garlic, ginger, soy sauce, soya beans (if using) and sesame oil. Set aside.

Put the chicken stock in a casserole or other heatproof container, followed by the crab claws, prawns and seasoned glass noodles. Cover with a lid and cook in a preheated steamer for about 10 minutes.

Use a pair of tongs to mix all the ingredients well, bringing the prawns and crab claws to the top. Sprinkle with the spring onion and pepper and steam for another 2–3 minutes.

Sprinkle with the chopped coriander leaves and serve, if you wish, with sweet chilli and garlic sauce.

Per serving: 501 kcals, 15.7g fat, 2.1g saturated fat, 27.4g total protein, 2g soya protein, 84mg calcium, 1.65g sodium

Rice with smoked halibut and thyme

The first time I made this I was trying to impress someone – and, boy, did it work! Smoked halibut is not cheap, but you only need a small quantity, so why not treat yourself. You could substitute undyed smoked haddock if necessary. **Serves 2**

- 1 tablespoon olive oil
- 165g (5½oz) rice, soaked in water for 30 minutes, and well drained
- 100g (3½oz) smoked halibut, cut into small pieces
- 65g (2½oz) white cabbage, roughly sliced and the layers separated
- 1 thyme sprig, leaves only
- 450ml (16fl oz) water
- Salt and pepper

Put the olive oil, rice and smoked halibut in a heavy-based pan and stir to mix well. Top with the cabbage, add the thyme and gently pour the water over the cabbage.

Cover the pan, bring to the boil and simmer for 15–20 minutes until all the liquid has been absorbed. Then stir gently and season with salt and pepper. Turn up the heat to high for about 15 seconds, still with the lid on the pan.

Remove from the heat, keeping the lid on, and leave the rice to stand for another 5–7 minutes before serving.

Per serving: 398 kcals, 6.7g fat, 0.8g saturated fat, 15.4g total protein, 38mg calcium, 0.48g sodium

Baked marinated sea bass with mashed sweet potatoes

Mashed sweet potatoes are a delicious alternative to the traditional mash, and you can achieve the same texture without having to use milk or butter. It goes extremely well with the rosemary-scented sea bass. **Serves 2**

4 garlic cloves, lightly crushed
10 mixed olives
Zest of 1 lemon
2 tablespoons extra virgin olive oil
Salt and black pepper
2 sea bass fillets
2 rosemary stems

For the mashed sweet potatoes
3 medium sweet potatoes, peeled and chopped
2 tablespoons extra virgin olive oil
Chopped parsley, to garnish

Preheat the oven to 200°C/400°F/gas mark 6.
In a large bowl, gently mix together the garlic, olives, lemon zest, olive oil and salt and pepper. Place the fish in an ovenproof dish and pour the mixture over it. Top with the rosemary and bake in the oven for 20 minutes.
Meanwhile, bring a large pan of water to the boil and add the sweet potato pieces. Reduce the heat and simmer until the potatoes are tender. Gently drain off the water and transfer the potato to a mixing bowl. Add the olive oil and mash well, seasoning with salt and pepper to taste.
Serve with the sea bass and the olive and rosemary sauce. Garnish with the parsley.

Per serving: 479 kcals, 26.8g fat, 4g saturated fat, 22.4g total protein, 195mg calcium, 0.57g sodium

Grilled salmon steaks with creamy lemon sauce

You will be surprised how delicious the sauce in this dish tastes, despite the usual cream being replaced by soya cream. Serve with steamed green vegetables or a fresh crispy salad. **Serves 2**

½ tablespoon olive oil
1 garlic clove, pounded with ½ fresh coriander root to make a paste
Salt and pepper
2 salmon fillets, weighing about 250g (8oz) each

For the sauce
½ tablespoon vegan margarine
2 garlic cloves, crushed
125ml (4fl oz) chicken stock
100ml (3½fl oz) soya cream
65ml (2½fl oz) freshly squeezed lemon juice
2 tablespoons finely chopped basil leaves

First make the sauce. Heat the margarine, add the garlic and stir-fry for a few minutes over a medium heat. Add the chicken stock, soya cream and lemon juice, then bring to the boil. Reduce the heat to low and simmer gently.
Meanwhile, preheat the grill to high and oil the grill rack. Season the garlic and coriander paste with salt and pepper to taste and spread it on both sides of the salmon. Grill the fish for about 3 minutes on each side or until it is cooked to your liking.
Transfer the salmon to individual serving plates. Add the basil to the sauce, season with salt and pepper and pour the sauce over the salmon.

Per serving: 381 kcals, 28.5g fat, 5.1g saturated fat, 28g total protein, 100mg calcium, 0.31g sodium

Monkfish skewers with coconut milk curry sauce

The texture of monkfish is like that of steak; it does not flake like other types of fish. This makes it extremely versatile – you can cook it in all kinds of ways and it keeps its shape. It is great for kebabs like these. Serves 2

- 2 tablespoons vegetable oil
- 1 tablespoon ready-made Thai red curry paste
- 2 tablespoons freshly squeezed lemon juice
- 2 teaspoons Thai fish sauce
- 1 teaspoon sugar
- 1 tablespoon chopped basil
- 450g (1lb) monkfish fillet, cut into 12 cubes
- Boiled rice (see page 49), to serve

For the sauce

- 1 tablespoon ready-made Thai red curry paste
- 100ml (3½fl oz) coconut milk
- ½ teaspoon sugar
- 6 basil leaves

Mix 1 tablespoon of the oil with the curry paste, lemon juice, fish sauce, sugar and basil in a large bowl. Add the cubes of fish, stirring so they are well coated, cover with clingfilm and place in the fridge to marinate for 15 minutes.

Preheat the grill to high and use the remaining oil to grease the grill rack.

Thread 6 cubes of monkfish on to each of 2 bamboo skewers, about 23cm (9in) long, which have been soaked in water. Place the skewers on the rack under the grill for about 3 minutes, turning them occasionally, until the fish has cooked through.

Meanwhile, put all the sauce ingredients except the basil leaves in a small saucepan and cook over medium heat, stirring frequently, until well mixed, smooth and heated through. Add the basil leaves, stir for another 15 seconds and the sauce is ready.

Serve the monkfish skewers with boiled rice and drizzle the rice with the coconut milk curry sauce.

Per serving: 333 kcals, 17.2g fat, 7.9g saturated fat, 37.2g total protein, 70mg calcium, 0.47g sodium

Dried chicken curry with warm pitta bread

One day I ran out of rice at home but I had some red curry with chicken left from the night before. I went to the shop and bought some pitta bread to eat with the curry. It turned out to be one of the best lunches I've had in years! Serves 2

- 1 tablespoon vegetable oil
- 1½ tablespoons ready-made Thai red curry paste
- 3 kaffir lime leaves, torn
- 100ml (3½fl oz) coconut cream
- 100ml (3½fl oz) soya milk
- 200g (7oz) boneless skinless chicken, thinly sliced along the grain
- 1½ teaspoons Thai fish sauce
- 1½ teaspoons sugar
- 75g (3oz) mangetout
- 2 large pitta breads, warmed
- 4 sweet basil leaves, chopped
- 1 red chilli, thinly sliced lengthways

Heat the oil in a wok over a low heat. Add the curry paste and lime leaves and stir-fry for about 15 seconds, taking care not to burn the mixture.

Slowly stir in the coconut cream and soya milk, then add the chicken, increase the heat to medium and cook until the chicken is cooked. If the sauce seems to be drying out, add a small amount of water to keep everything moist, but do not make the sauce too thin. Season with the fish sauce and sugar. Add the mangetout and stir around for a minute or so.

Pile the dried chicken curry into the warmed pitta breads and sprinkle with the basil leaves and chilli slices before serving.

Per serving: 448 kcals, 14.8g fat, 10.3g saturated fat, 34.9g total protein, 1.5g soya protein, 213mg calcium, 0.56g sodium

Pan-fried chicken breast with creamy basil sauce

Skinless chicken breasts are relatively low in fat and therefore go well with a richer kind of sauce. This sauce is creamy without using dairy cream, and is, in fact, quite light. Serve with vegetables of your choice. **Serves 2**

1 tablespoon plain flour
Salt and pepper
2 large skinless boneless chicken breasts
2 teaspoons olive oil
2 teaspoons vegan margarine
2 basil sprigs, to garnish

For the basil cream sauce
2 teaspoons vegan margarine
1 garlic clove, crushed
4 tablespoons chicken stock or water
65ml (2½fl oz) soya cream
30ml (1fl oz) freshly squeezed lemon juice
1 tablespoon finely chopped basil leaves

Put the flour in a bowl and season with salt and pepper. Coat the chicken breasts in the flour, shaking off any excess.
Heat the oil and margarine in a frying pan, add the chicken and cook over medium heat for 5 minutes on each side or until golden and cooked through. Remove from the pan and keep warm.
Meanwhile, make the sauce. Heat the margarine in the same pan, add the garlic and cook for a couple of minutes. Add the chicken stock or water, soya cream and lemon juice, then bring to the boil. Lower the heat, add the chopped basil leaves and season with salt and pepper to taste.
Place each chicken breast on a serving plate and pour over the sauce. Garnish each with a sprig of basil and serve.

Per serving: 349 kcals, 18.7g fat, 3.5g saturated fat, 38.2g total protein, 63mg calcium, 0.32g sodium

Steamed chicken and ginger rice

This has been a favourite dish of mine since I was eight years old. I just love the aroma that fills the kitchen as you cook the rice. You must eat it with chilled cucumber slices, otherwise it's like having toast without butter and jam! Serves 2

1 teaspoon vegetable oil
1 teaspoon crushed garlic
450g (1lb) rice, washed and well drained
½ chicken, about 500g (18oz), half the skin trimmed off
1.2 litres (2 pints) water
½ teaspoon salt
2 fresh coriander roots, pounded
A thumb-size piece of fresh root ginger, cut in half and lightly pounded (do not peel)
Chilled cucumber slices
Coriander leaves, to garnish

For the sauce
1 teaspoon fresh ginger root paste
1 teaspoon finely chopped garlic
½ teaspoon sugar
3 bird's eye chillies, finely chopped
2 tablespoons fermented soya beans
1 tablespoon chicken stock

To season the soup
½ tablespoon light soy sauce, or to taste
Pinch of ground white pepper
2 spring onions, finely chopped

In a frying pan, heat the oil and fry in the garlic until it releases its aroma. Add the rice grains and fry with the garlic and oil until mixed well, then set aside.

Put the chicken in a saucepan with the water and bring to the boil. Simmer for about 30 minutes until you have a well-flavoured stock and the chicken is cooked. Reserve a tablespoon for the sauce.

Steam the garlic rice in an electric rice cooker using 850ml (1½ pints) of the chicken stock and adding the pounded coriander roots and ginger. If you don't have a rice cooker, place the rice, stock, coriander roots and ginger in a heavy-based pan, cover with a tight-fitting lid and bring to the boil. Turn down the heat to low and simmer for 15–20 minutes until all the stock is absorbed. Remove the pan from the heat and leave to stand for 5–7 minutes, still with the lid on.

To make the sauce, mix all the ingredients for the sauce together, stir well and set aside.

Remove the chicken from the remainder of the stock. Discard the bones and chop the meat into small pieces. Keep the chicken stock to make a mild soup to accompany the rice (see below).

Scoop the cooked rice on to a serving plate, discarding the ginger lumps and coriander roots, then arrange the chicken on top along with the cucumber slices and a sprinkling of coriander leaves. Serve the sauce in a separate dish.

Reheat the chicken stock, season with the light soy sauce and ground white pepper, sprinkle with the chopped spring onions and serve with the rice.

Per serving: 494 kcals, 7g fat, 1.4g saturated fat, 38.8g total protein, 4g soya protein, 37mg calcium, 1.53g sodium

Grilled curried sausage with herbal accompaniments

Ready-made sausages often contain dairy products, so here is an easy recipe for making your own – Thai-style. Serve with the mash and 'gravy' on the right for my interpretation of the classic bangers and mash! **Serves 4**

- 500g (18oz) minced pork
- 10g (½oz) lemongrass, finely chopped
- 10g (½oz) galangal, pounded to a paste
- 4 kaffir lime leaves, finely chopped
- 2 red chillies and 2 garlic cloves, blended together in a blender or pestle and mortar
- 2–3 tablespoons ready-made Thai red curry paste
- ¾ tablespoon sugar
- ½ tablespoon salt
- 1 teaspoon ground turmeric
- Coriander sprigs, to garnish
- 6–8 bird's eye chillies, sliced
- 6cm (2½in) piece of fresh ginger root, peeled and cut into thin matchsticks

Preheat the grill to high.

Mix the pork well with the next 8 ingredients. Using your hands, form small quantities of the mixture into sausage shapes.

Place the sausages under the grill for about 10–15 minutes or until the pork is well cooked, turning occasionally.

Serve the sausages garnished with a few coriander sprigs, the bird's eye chillies and ginger. Accompany with the pan-fried mashed potatoes, drizzled with the creamy green curry sauce (see right).

Per serving (without mashed potatoes and sauce): 269 kcals, 15.8g fat, 4.5g saturated fat, 25.4g total protein, 43mg calcium, 1.07g sodium

Pan-fried mashed potatoes with green curry sauce

- Salt and pepper
- 2 large potatoes, peeled and cut into small chunks
- 1 teaspoon chopped fresh ginger and 1 teaspoon chopped fresh coriander root, pounded together to make a fine paste
- 1 tablespoon vegan margarine
- ½ tablespoon vegetable oil
- 2 teaspoons ready-made Thai green curry paste
- 150ml (¼ pint) soya cream

Bring a pan of salted water to the boil and add the potatoes. Cook until tender, then drain. Mash the potatoes with half of the ginger and coriander root paste and season with salt and pepper to taste.

Brush a non-stick flat-bottomed frying pan with a little margarine and heat. Put a large scoop of mashed potatoes in the middle of the pan and use a spatula to flatten it. Pan-fry until slightly browned and crisp, then carefully turn it over to cook the other side in the same way. Repeat the process with the remaining mashed potatoes.

To make the sauce, heat the oil in a frying pan over medium heat. Stir in the remainder of the ginger and coriander root paste, taking care not to burn it. Add the green curry paste and stir for 10–15 seconds before pouring in the soya cream. Gently stir to blend all the ingredients and leave to simmer for 2–3 minutes until the sauce has thickened slightly.

Per serving (mashed potatoes and sauce only): 208 kcals, 11.9g fat, 1.8g saturated fat, 3.9g total protein, 46mg calcium, 0.19g sodium

Grilled marinated lamb chops with fragrant spices

I'm not that familiar with lamb because I was not brought up eating it on a regular basis. However, I enjoy this dish which partners the meat with other aromatic ingredients and a fresh vegetable sauce. **Serves 2**

- 1 teaspoon cumin seeds, lightly toasted and finely ground
- 2.5cm (1in) piece of fresh ginger root, peeled and finely chopped
- 2 shallots, chopped
- 2 garlic cloves, chopped
- 1 lemongrass stalk, chopped
- 1 tablespoon sugar
- ½ teaspoon salt
- 1 tablespoon vegetable oil, plus a little extra for blending
- 2 double lamb loin chops, trimmed of excess fat

For the sauce

- 25g (1oz) vegan margarine
- 200g (7½oz) leeks, thinly sliced
- 80ml soya cream
- 100g (3½oz) frozen peas
- Salt and pepper

Put the cumin powder, ginger, shallots, garlic, lemongrass, sugar and salt in a food processor and whizz to a smooth paste, adding a tiny amount of oil to help the mixture turn.

Heat the oil in a pan and stir-fry the paste over a low heat to release the fragrance, then remove from the pan and allow to cool.

Rub the paste all over the lamb chops and leave, covered, in the fridge to marinate for 30 minutes.

Meanwhile, make the sauce. Heat the margarine in a frying pan and fry the leeks for 10 minutes over medium heat until they are soft. Add the soya cream and bring to the boil. Lower the heat and add the peas, season with salt and pepper and continue to cook for a further 4 minutes.

Preheat the grill to high. Grill the chops for about 3–4 minutes on each side or less if you like your lamb quite rare. Serve with the leek and pea sauce.

Per serving: 531 kcals, 35g fat, 9.2g saturated fat, 36g total protein, 131mg calcium, 0.71g sodium

Minced beef curry with jacket potato

Have you ever heard of Bolognese sauce on jacket potatoes? Well, now you have! This is my way of making it, but the meat sauce is more fiery and I think, tastier than the usual version. **Serves 2**

- 2 large baking potatoes, scrubbed
- 1 tablespoon vegetable oil
- 200g (7oz) lean minced beef
- 1½ tablespoons ready-made Thai red curry paste
- 75ml (3fl oz) coconut milk
- 75ml (3fl oz) soya cream
- 1½ teaspoons Thai fish sauce
- 1½ teaspoons sugar
- 6 basil leaves

Preheat the oven to 180°C/350°F/gas mark 4.

Wrap the potatoes in foil and bake on the middle shelf of the oven for about 2 hours or until cooked through.

Heat the oil in a wok over a medium heat. Add the minced beef and fry, stirring often, until the beef is half cooked. Add the curry paste, followed by the coconut milk and soya cream and stir to mix well. Season with the fish sauce and sugar. Reduce the heat to low and simmer for a couple of minutes. Add the basil leaves and give it one more good stir.

Unwrap the potatoes, split them open and serve with the curry sauce poured over them.

Per serving: 554 kcals, 31g fat, 11g saturated fat, 29g total protein, 95mg calcium, 0.78g sodium

Rosemary cheeseburger with plantain chips and tomato salsa

You don't have to go without a cheeseburger just because you're following a dairy-free diet. This one is much tastier than the burger-bar version – and far healthier. Serves 2

1 slice of white bread, crust removed
175g (6oz) lean minced beef
1 egg yolk, beaten
2 slices of soya cheese
2 sesame bread baps
Handful of spinach leaves

For the plantain chips

1 plantain
100g (3½oz) plain flour
1 tablespoon vegetable oil

For the tomato salsa

1 tablespoon olive oil
2 rosemary sprigs, leaves only
2 garlic cloves, finely chopped
2 plum tomatoes, chopped into small pieces
Juice of ½ lemon
Salt and pepper

Make the salsa first of all. In a frying pan, heat the olive oil and fry the rosemary leaves together with the garlic until they release their fragrance. Stir in the tomatoes, cook for another minute and season with the lemon juice and salt and pepper to taste. Set aside.

Tear the slice of white bread into small pieces, place in a food processor and process into crumbs. In a large bowl, use your hands to mix the beef, egg yolk and breadcrumbs together, then season with pepper.

Preheat the grill to high. Shape the mixture into 2 even-sized burgers not more than 1cm (½in) thick. Cook the burgers under the grill for 3 minutes on each side or until cooked to your liking. Put a slice of cheese on top of each burger and continue to grill until the cheese has melted, then keep warm.

Split open the bread baps and place them cut side down on the griddle pan or under the grill to toast them lightly.

Meanwhile, peel the plantain and thinly slice across at an angle. Coat the pieces with the plain flour. Heat a frying pan, brush with the oil and fry the plantain pieces in batches for a minute each side, turning once, until golden brown. Set aside.

Arrange some spinach leaves on the bottom half of each bap and top with a burger and some tomato salsa. Cover with the top half of each bap and serve alongside the plantain chips.

Per serving: 868 kcals, 34.7g fat, 8.1g saturated fat, 40.9g total protein, 4.5g soya protein, 376mg calcium, 0.72g sodium

4 Main Courses

Polenta with wild mushrooms and spaghetti squash *This wonderful combination of flavours and textures makes a great vegetarian main course that is free from dairy products. Spaghetti squash is an interesting-looking vegetable that should be used more often.* Serves 4

1.8 litres (3 pints) water
Salt and ground black pepper
200g (7oz) coarse polenta
50g (2oz) vegan margarine
½ spaghetti squash, about 500g (18oz), deseeded

For the mushrooms
4 tablespoons olive oil
1 garlic clove, chopped
500g (18oz) wild or cultivated flat mushrooms, quartered
1 tablespoon chopped oregano, plus a few sprigs
150ml (¼ pint) dry white wine

Bring the water to the boil in a large saucepan with 1 teaspoon salt. Gradually add the polenta, letting it run through your fingers in a stream and stirring constantly to prevent lumps forming. Simmer for 30–35 minutes, continuing to stir, until the mixture comes away from the sides of the pan.

Stir in the margarine and add pepper to taste. While the polenta is still hot, spread it on a dampened baking sheet or wooden board to a thickness of about 1cm (½in). Leave for an hour or so or until softly set.

Meanwhile, cook the spaghetti squash in boiling water until just tender. Using a fork, rake out the spaghetti-like strands of flesh and keep warm.

To cook the mushrooms, heat the olive oil in a pan and add the garlic, mushrooms and chopped oregano. Cook for a few minutes, then add the wine, raise the heat and continue to cook until the wine has almost completely evaporated. Season to taste and keep warm.

Preheat a griddle, cut the polenta into triangles and griddle on both sides until lightly charred.

Serve the polenta immediately with strings of spaghetti squash and the mushrooms.

Per serving: 434 kcals, 23.9g fat, 4g saturated fat, 7.9g total protein, 52mg calcium, 0.64g sodium

Stuffed peppers with aromatic rice

A new twist on a classic theme: the filling for these peppers is deliciously flavoured with garlic, chilli, basil and soy sauce. You can use red, green, orange or yellow peppers or a mixture of colours – your choice! Serves 4

4 red, green, orange or yellow peppers
4 tablespoons vegetable oil
4 garlic cloves, pounded with 2 fresh chillies to make a coarse paste
80g (3oz) cooked rice (see page 49)
100g (3½oz) onion, diced
100g (3½oz) spring greens, thinly sliced
80g (3oz) broccoli, stalks thinly sliced, florets cut into bite-size pieces
50g (2oz) mangetout, topped and tailed
4 teaspoons light soy sauce
1 teaspoon dark soy sauce
2 teaspoons white sugar
Salt, to taste
½ handful of holy basil leaves
1 fresh red chilli, chopped

Preheat the oven to 190°C/375°F/gas mark 5.

Cut the tops off the peppers and reserve them to use as 'lids'. Scoop out the core and seeds and set aside.

Heat a wok or frying pan over a medium heat, then add the oil. Add the garlic and chilli paste and stir for a couple of seconds until it releases its aroma. (By heating the wok first, you ensure that the oil won't be so hot that it burns the paste when you add it.) Immediately stir in the rice, followed by the onion, spring greens, broccoli and mangetout. Season with the soy sauces, sugar and salt, stirring to distribute the brown colour from the soy sauces evenly. Add the holy basil leaves and chopped chilli and stir for a few seconds.

Stuff the rice mixture tightly into the peppers. Brush the base of a shallow baking dish or roasting tin with a little oil and stand the stuffed peppers in it. Replace the pepper 'lids' and bake in the oven for about 20 minutes until the peppers are soft but still whole. Serve hot.

Per serving: 437 kcals, 24.5g fat, 2.6g saturated fat, 10.3g total protein, 194mg calcium, 1.11g sodium

Baked leeks with fennel and potatoes

I tend to use leeks as I do spring onions, but because leeks are thicker and firmer they are more suitable for baking. I cannot think of any Thai dish that uses leeks; I will have to create one when I have a moment! **Serves 4**

400g (14oz) fennel bulbs
400g (14oz) new potatoes
225g (8oz) leeks, sliced into 7.5cm (3in) lengths
100ml (3½fl oz) olive oil
3 tablespoons vegan margarine, melted
25ml water
1 lemon
4 thyme sprigs
2 large red onions, cut into rings 7mm (⅓in) thick
Salt and pepper

Preheat the oven to 200°C/400°F/gas mark 6.

Quarter the fennel bulbs and cut the new potatoes in half. Place, cut side up, with the leeks in a large roasting tin, then drizzle with the olive oil, melted margarine and the small amount of water.

Halve the lemon and squeeze the juice from both halves on to the vegetables, then add the squeezed lemon halves to the roasting tin as well. Add the thyme and cover with a dampened sheet of non-stick baking parchment.

Cook in the oven for about 20–25 minutes or until the vegetables are tender. About 10 minutes before they are ready, add the red onions to the roasting tin and continue to bake until everything is tender. Season with salt and pepper before serving.

Per serving: 387 kcals, 29.7g fat, 4.5g saturated fat, 4.9g total protein, 80mg calcium, 0.18g sodium

Carrot and pumpkin risotto

This is a very colourful dish and tastes quite sweet because of the natural sweetness of the carrots and pumpkin. The texture of the pumpkin combined with the rice makes this risotto quite substantial.

Serves 4

2 litres (3½ pints) vegetable stock
25g (1oz) vegan margarine
3 tablespoons olive oil
2 garlic cloves
1 red onion, finely chopped
200g (7oz) carrots, chopped
500g (18oz) pumpkin, peeled, deseeded and chopped
450g (1lb) risotto rice
Salt and ground black pepper
½ handful of basil leaves, finely chopped

Bring the stock to the boil in a pan, then reduce the heat and keep at a low simmer.

Heat the margarine and olive oil in a large, heavy-based saucepan over a medium heat. Add the garlic and onion and stir-fry for a couple of minutes, taking care not to burn the garlic. Add the carrots and pumpkin and cook until soft. Add the rice and stir for a minute with the rest of ingredients until well coated.

Add a ladleful of hot stock and simmer, stirring, until it has been absorbed. Continue to repeat this process, adding a ladleful of hot stock at a time, until the rice is tender but retaining a bite. Season to taste with salt and pepper and stir in the basil leaves.

Remove from the heat, cover and leave to stand for about 3–4 minutes. Spoon into warm bowls and serve immediately.

Per serving: 552 kcals, 14.9g fat, 2.4g saturated fat, 12.7g total protein, 132mg calcium, 0.81g sodium

Massaman curry with Quorn and vegetables

One of the few Thai curries that are garnished with coriander instead of sweet basil, which shows that its roots are in Muslim countries that are neighbours of Thailand. If you can't find Massaman curry paste, use Thai red curry paste. **Serves 4**

1 tablespoon vegetable oil
4 tablespoons Massaman curry paste or Thai red curry paste
310g (11oz) Quorn chunks
200ml (7fl oz) coconut milk
300ml (½ pint) soya cream
2 large potatoes, peeled and each cut into 4–5 chunks
1 onion, coarsely sliced
1 tablespoon roasted peanuts
4 cardamom seeds, roasted (if using red curry paste)
2 x 2.5cm (1in) cinnamon sticks, roasted (if using red curry paste)
2 tablespoons tamarind juice or 1½ tablespoons freshly squeezed lemon juice
3 tablespoons palm sugar or 1¼ tablespoons sugar
1½ tablespoons Thai fish sauce or salt to taste (for vegetarians)
½ handful of coriander leaves, to garnish
Naan bread or cooked rice (see page 49), to serve

For the crispy shallots

4 shallots, thinly sliced
1 tablespoon vegetable oil

First make the crispy shallots. Heat the oil in a wok over medium heat. Add the shallot slices and fry, stirring, until they turn golden brown and crisp. Remove from the pan and drain well on kitchen paper. Set aside.

To make the curry, heat the oil in a wok over a low heat. Add the curry paste and stir-fry for about 15 seconds, taking care not to let it burn. Add the Quorn chunks and stir-fry, constantly tossing and turning, for 1 minute.

Stir in the coconut milk and soya cream and simmer, stirring, for 5 minutes, then add the potatoes, onion, peanuts, cardamom seeds and cinnamon sticks (if using). Season with the tamarind or lemon juice, sugar and fish sauce or salt. Leave the curry to simmer for about 20 minutes, or until the potatoes are cooked through and oil starts appearing on the surface of the sauce.

Transfer the curry to a serving bowl and garnish with the crispy shallots and coriander leaves. Serve alongside naan bread or rice.

Per serving: 536 kcals, 34.9g fat, 10.4g saturated fat, 19.7g total protein, 153mg calcium, 1.01g sodium

Jungle curry with lychees and courgettes

Jungle curry, so called because it was traditionally made with any vegetables that country dwellers had to hand, is actually my most favourite curry of all. It is great for the waistline as well as being very healthy. **Serves 4**

- 4 tablespoons ready-made Thai red curry paste
- 1 teaspoon grated kaffir lime zest
- 1½ tablespoons vegetable oil
- 5 kaffir lime leaves, torn
- 700ml (1¼ pints) vegetable stock or water
- 400g (14oz) tin lychees, drained and 200ml (7fl oz) of the syrup reserved
- 310g (11oz) butternut squash, peeled and cut into chunks
- 2 large courgettes
- 7cm (2¾in) piece of aromatic ginger *(gra-chai)*, cut into thin matchsticks
- 1 tablespoon fresh green peppercorns (see page 120)
- 4 tablespoons Thai fish sauce
- 1 teaspoon sugar
- ½ handful of holy basil leaves
- 1 fresh green chilli, thinly sliced lengthways
- 1 fresh red chilli, thinly sliced lengthways
- Boiled rice (see page 49), to serve

Begin by enhancing the ready-made curry paste. Use a pestle and mortar to pound the grated lime zest and curry paste together. Heat the oil in a wok over a low heat, then add the paste and stir-fry for about 15 seconds until the paste releases its aroma, taking care not to burn it. Add the lime leaves and stir for a further 10 seconds.

Add the vegetable stock or water to the wok together with the reserved lychee syrup and bring to the boil, constantly stirring to make sure the curry paste is well mixed with the liquid and there are no lumps.

Lower the heat to medium, add the butternut squash and cook for 3–4 minutes or until it is tender. Add the courgettes, lychees, ginger and green peppercorns. Season with the fish sauce and sugar and leave to cook for a further 2 minutes.

Just before serving, add most of the holy basil leaves and most of the sliced chillies and give the curry one last stir. Transfer to a serving bowl and garnish with the remaining basil and chillies. Serve with boiled rice.

Per serving: 217 kcals, 8g fat, 0.6g saturated fat, 6.8g total protein, 134mg calcium, 1.62g sodium

Aubergine with garlic and chilli

This dish goes nicely with most types of pasta or can be served on toasted bruschetta. It also works well as a pizza topping, but is better without the usual cheese, so it's ideal for people who are reducing or eliminating dairy products from their diet. **Serves 4**

- 1 large aubergine
- 1 tablespoon vegetable oil
- 8 baby tomatoes, halved
- 2 garlic cloves, pounded with 1 fresh red chilli to make a paste
- ½ teaspoon sugar
- Salt, to taste
- 4 tablespoons vegetable stock or water
- 1 fresh red chilli, sliced lengthways
- ½ handful of basil leaves

Slice the aubergine lengthways into long flat pieces and dip the slices in cold water, then drain on kitchen paper. Cook in a frying pan over low heat without any oil, turning once, until cooked but still firm. Drain off any excess water, and keep the aubergine slices warm.

Heat the oil in the same pan, add the tomatoes together with garlic and chilli paste and stir-fry for a few seconds, taking care not to let the paste burn. Reduce the heat, season with the sugar and salt to taste and pour in the stock or water. Simmer for about 30 seconds or until the sauce has thickened slightly. Stir in most of the sliced chilli and most of the basil leaves and heat for a few seconds.

Drizzle the sauce over the cooked aubergines and serve garnished with the remaining chilli slices and basil leaves.

Per serving: 54 kcals, 3.4g fat, 0.3g saturated fat, 1.6g total protein, 20mg calcium, 0.12g sodium

Stir-fried assorted mushrooms and baby corn with spring onions

I like all kinds of mushrooms and it really surprises me that there are quite a few people who are allergic to them. What a pity! This dish can be served with boiled egg noodles or steamed rice. **Serves 4**

- 2 tablespoons vegetable oil
- 4 garlic cloves, crushed
- 125g (4½oz) oyster mushrooms, trimmed
- 65g (2½oz) dried straw mushrooms, soaked in warm water until soft, squeezed dry and sliced into thin strips
- 80g (3oz) button mushrooms, quartered
- 30g (1¼oz) dried jelly mushrooms (ear mushrooms), soaked in warm water until soft and squeezed dry
- 80g (3oz) baby corn
- 4 tablespoons water
- 1 tablespoon Thai fish sauce
- 1 tablespoon light soy sauce
- ½ teaspoon sugar
- 2 spring onions, cut into 2.5cm (1in) lengths
- 1 tablespoon tapioca flour, mixed to a paste with 2–3 tablespoons cold water
- 1 tablespoon sesame oil
- Pinch of ground white pepper
- Coriander leaves, to garnish

Heat the oil in a wok over a medium heat. Add the crushed garlic and stir around for a few seconds until it releases its fragrance. Add all the mushrooms together with the baby corn and stir for a minute or two, then add the water and bring to the boil, stirring constantly.

Reduce the heat to medium and season with the fish sauce, soy sauce and sugar. Stir in the spring onions. Add the tapioca flour paste and stir until the sauce thickens to the consistency of gravy.

Serve sprinkled with ground white pepper and coriander leaves.

Per serving: 177 kcals, 8.9g fat, 1.1g saturated fat, 4.7g total protein, 51mg calcium, 0.6g sodium

Poached eggs topped with onion and tomatoes

When I was a little girl, my grandmother told me, with a straight face, that this dish was called 'poor man's eggs'. I realise now this is because the ingredients are quite cheap, but it is no less enjoyable for that. **Serves 4**

Vegetable oil, for frying
1 onion, thinly sliced into rings
3 large plum tomatoes, diced
3 large new potatoes, diced
1 large carrot, diced
2 tablespoons water
1½ tablespoons Thai fish sauce
1 teaspoon distilled malt vinegar
1 teaspoon sugar
8 small eggs
Pinch of ground white pepper

Heat a little oil in a frying pan, add the onion rings and fry, stirring occasionally, until lightly browned. Stir in the rest of the vegetables, cook for a couple of minutes and add the water. Cover and simmer until the carrots and potatoes are cooked but still slightly firm – be careful not to overcook them. Season with the fish sauce, vinegar and sugar and keep warm.

To cook the eggs, bring a pan of water to the boil. Gently break in the eggs one by one (you will probably have to prepare them in 3 batches). Cook them until the egg whites form (about 4 minutes) or to suit your taste. When the eggs are cooked, use a slotted spoon to lift them gently out of the pan and on to plate. Keep warm while you cook the remaining 5 eggs in the same way.

Carefully arrange the poached eggs on a large oval serving plate. Pour the vegetable sauce over them, sprinkle with the pepper and serve.

Per serving: 347 kcals, 21.8g fat, 4.7g saturated fat, 19.3g total protein, 111mg calcium, 0.65g sodium

Seasonal vegetables with couscous

Here I have used couscous instead of the (for me) more usual rice. They do taste very similar but I find couscous has a much finer texture and is not as filling as rice, so it's a good partner for mixed vegetables. **Serves 4**

350g (12oz) couscous
600ml (1 pint) boiling water
110g (4oz) baby carrots, chopped
1 red pepper, deseeded and thinly sliced
110g (4oz) sugar snap peas
4 baby leeks, sliced
110g (4oz) sweetcorn kernels
65ml (2½fl oz) lemon juice
2 tablespoons olive oil
Salt and pepper
1 tablespoon chopped mint

Put the couscous in a large bowl and cover with the boiling water. Leave to stand for 10 minutes or until all the water has been absorbed, then fluff up the couscous grains with a fork.

Cook the carrots in lightly salted boiling water for 2 minutes, then add the red pepper, sugar snap peas, leeks and sweetcorn kernels and continue to cook for a further 3 minutes. Drain well before adding to the couscous.

Add the lemon juice and oil to the bowl and stir in carefully. Season with salt and pepper to taste, gently stir in the chopped mint and serve.

Per serving: 308 kcals, 7.3g fat, 1g saturated fat, 7.9g total protein, 54mg calcium, 0.11g sodium

Fusilli in lime and coconut milk sauce

This is a workable fusion, not confusion! I would have not dared make this dish without first using my Italian friends as guinea pigs. Great combination. If you are looking for a lower fat content, try diluting the coconut milk. **Serves 3**

350g (12oz) dried fusilli pasta
Salt, to taste
1 teaspoon grated lime zest
Coriander leaves, to garnish

For the sauce
300ml (½ pint) coconut milk
1 lemongrass stalk, lightly crushed
1 fresh coriander root, lightly crushed
2 kaffir lime leaves
150ml (¼ pint) water
1½ teaspoons sugar
1cm (½in) piece of galangal, thinly sliced
50g (2oz) oyster mushrooms
4 small dried chillies, stems removed
1½ tablespoons freshly squeezed lime juice

Cook the fusilli in a large pan of boiling salted water, according to the packet instructions, until tender but still firm to the bite.

Meanwhile, put the coconut milk in a saucepan over a high heat and bring to the boil. Add the lemongrass stalk, coriander root and lime leaves. Add the measured water, lower the heat and simmer for 10 minutes. Strain to discard all the flavourings.

Season the sauce with salt to taste and the sugar and stir well. Add the galangal, mushrooms and dried chillies, then bring to the boil. Add the lime juice.

Remove from the heat, add the cooked drained fusilli and stir to make sure that the pasta is well coated with the sauce. Transfer to individual serving plates, sprinkle with the lime zest and garnish with coriander leaves.

Per serving: 588 kcals, 18.7g fat, 14.3g saturated fat, 16g total protein, 73mg calcium, 0.59g sodium

Macaroni with roast cherry tomatoes

This is a little like macaroni cheese, but without the cheese! It's so tasty that I don't think you will miss the cheese; however, if you must have some, you can add grated vegan cheese to the sauce. **Serves 4**

175g (6oz) cherry tomatoes
1 tablespoon olive oil
Salt and ground black pepper
225g (8oz) dried macaroni
50g (2oz) vegan margarine
40g (1½oz) plain flour
500ml (18fl oz) vegetable stock
1 tablespoon Dijon mustard
2 eggs, beaten

Preheat the oven to 220°C/425°F/gas mark 7.

Place the cherry tomatoes in a 2-litre (3½–pint) ovenproof dish. Drizzle over the olive oil and season with salt and pepper. Roast the tomatoes for about 15 minutes until they have softened slightly and the skins have split. Set aside.

Meanwhile, cook the macaroni in a large pan of boiling salted water according to the packet instructions or until tender but firm to the bite. Drain and set aside.

Melt the margarine in a saucepan, add the flour and cook for about 20 seconds. Slowly add the vegetable stock, stirring constantly until the sauce is smooth, and bring to the boil to thicken the sauce. Add the mustard and season with salt and pepper to taste. Allow to cool slightly.

Mix the eggs into the sauce and stir in well, then add the cooked macaroni. Return the pan to a low heat and stir well for about 5–6 minutes until the macaroni is heated through and the eggs are cooked – but take care not to scramble the eggs.

Transfer the pasta to the ovenproof dish containing the tomatoes and gently mix together. Bake in the oven for about 15–20 minutes until golden brown. Serve hot.

Per serving: 410 kcals, 18g fat, 3.6g saturated fat, 12.7g total protein, 71mg calcium, 0.52g sodium

Tagliatelle with oyster mushrooms and walnuts

This dish is so simple to prepare, yet the white wine and soya cream give it a touch of luxury. The resulting creamy sauce is just perfect for those ideal partners, mushrooms and walnuts. **Serves 4**

3 tablespoons olive oil
225g (8oz) oyster mushrooms, torn into pieces
2 garlic cloves, crushed
1 onion, finely chopped
50g (2oz) walnuts, roughly chopped
150ml (¼ pint) dry white wine
4 tablespoons soya cream
2 tablespoons chopped rosemary leaves, plus 2 sprigs to garnish
1 small leek, finely chopped
Salt, to taste
225g (8oz) dried tagliatelle

Heat the oil in a frying pan and fry the mushrooms together with the garlic and onion until the mushrooms soften, then add the walnuts and fry, stirring, for another 3 minutes.

Pour in the wine and soya cream and add the chopped rosemary and leek. Simmer for a few minutes until the leek is tender. Season with salt to taste. Keep warm.

Meanwhile, cook the pasta in a large pan of boiling salted water, following the instruction on the packet, until tender but firm to the bite. Drain well. Divide the pasta between serving plates, top with the creamy sauce and garnish with the rosemary sprigs.

Per serving: 435 kcals, 20.9g fat, 2.6g saturated fat, 11.1g total protein, 84mg calcium, 0.21g sodium

Vegetable lasagne

You can still enjoy a creamy lasagne even though you are committed to dairy-free eating. This vegetarian version uses soya milk and cheese and tastes every bit as good as the usual sort, with just the right kind of gungy texture! **Serves 4**

- 250g (9oz) dried lasagne
- 2 tablespoons extra virgin olive oil
- 3 garlic cloves, crushed
- 1 red onion, finely chopped
- 1 aubergine, sliced into rounds about 5mm (¼in) thick
- 1 red or yellow pepper, deseeded and diced
- 400g (14oz) tin chopped tomatoes
- 1 courgette, sliced into rounds about 1cm (½in) thick
- 1 tablespoon tomato purée
- 200ml (7fl oz) vegetable stock
- 50g (2oz) soya cheese, finely grated
- 25g (1oz) breadcrumbs

For the white sauce

- 40g (1½oz) vegan margarine
- 25g (1oz) plain flour
- 500ml (18fl oz) soya milk
- 2 teaspoons Dijon mustard
- Salt and pepper
- 2 tablespoons chopped oregano

If using the type of dried lasagne sheets for which the instruction says 'no need to precook', I still like to precook them as I then find it easier to arrange or tear them if I need to. Bring a large pan of lightly salted water to the boil, add the lasagne sheets, stir gently and return to the boil. Boil for 10 minutes and drain well. Rinse the lasagne sheets with cold water to prevent them from sticking together. Set aside.

Heat the oil in a large saucepan over a medium heat and fry the garlic and onion for a few minutes. Stir in the aubergine and red or yellow pepper and sauté for another 10 minutes, stirring occasionally. Add the tomatoes, cougette, tomato purée and stock, cover and leave to simmer for a further 7–8 minutes until the vegetables are just tender – take care not to overcook. Remove from the heat and set aside.

Preheat the oven to 200°C/400°F/gas mark 6.

To make the white sauce, melt the margarine in a pan, add the flour and cook over a medium heat for a couple of minutes, stirring constantly. Gently add the soya milk and mustard, then bring to the boil, continuing to stir well until the sauce thickens, Season with salt and pepper to taste and stir in the oregano.

Spread half of the vegetable mixture in a rectangular ovenproof dish, drizzle about 2–3 tablespoons of white sauce over it and place a layer of lasagne sheets evenly on top. Repeat the process until you have used up all the vegetable mixture, making sure you end the process with white sauce on top of the last layer of lasagne sheets.

Mix together the soya cheese and breadcrumbs and sprinkle evenly over the top of the dish. Bake in the oven for about 30–35 minutes until the top is golden brown. Serve hot.

Per serving: 524 kcals, 21.6g fat, 3.3g saturated fat, 18.3g total protein, 5g soya protein, 158mg calcium, 0.57g sodium

Steamed egg with spring onions and shrimps

This is one of the healthiest ways to make an egg dish. It tastes like delicious soft white tofu and is very delicate and light in texture. It is also great made without shrimps if you are a vegetarian. **Serves** 4

8 medium eggs
250ml (9fl oz) water
150g (5oz) cooked shrimps
2 tablespoons Thai fish sauce
2 teaspoons sugar
10 shallots, thinly sliced
4 spring onions, finely chopped
Boiled rice (see page 49), to serve

To garnish
2 teaspoons crispy garlic (see page 75)
½ handful of coriander leaves
Ground white pepper

Preheat a steamer on high until the water boils.
Beat the eggs with the water in a shallow bowl that fits inside the steamer, then stir in the shrimps, fish sauce, sugar, shallots and spring onions.
Put the bowl of egg mixture in the steamer, close the lid and steam for 15–20 minutes until the egg is set and firm.
Garnish with the crispy garlic, coriander leaves and a sprinkling of white pepper. Serve with boiled rice.

Per serving: 230 kcals, 13.5g fat, 3.3g saturated fat, 23.1g total protein, 193mg calcium, 2.16g sodium

Tiger prawns with celery and pine nuts

I adore pine nuts and believe they should be used more in all types of cooking. They have a unique flavour and character, especially when toasted. In this stir-fry recipe I have used them instead of the usual cashew nuts or roasted peanuts. **Serves 4**

2 tablespoons pine nuts
2 tablespoons vegetable oil
2 garlic cloves, crushed
250g (9oz) raw black tiger prawns, peeled, deveined and de-headed; tails left on
100g (3½oz) celery (preferably Chinese), chopped, including the leaves
2 tablespoons Thai fish sauce
1 tablespoon sugar
Ground white pepper
Coriander leaves, to garnish
Boiled rice (see page 49), or egg noodles, to serve

Toast the pine nuts in a dry frying pan without any oil until golden. Set aside.
Heat the oil in a wok over a medium heat. Add the garlic and stir for 30 seconds, taking care not to burn it, then add the prawns and stir until they are half cooked.
Add the celery and continue to cook for 30–40 seconds. Season with the fish sauce, toasted pine nuts and sugar, constantly stirring to blend in the seasoning well.
Sprinkle with ground white pepper and garnish with coriander leaves. Serve hot with boiled rice or egg noodles.

Per serving: 163 kcals, 10.1g fat, 1.1g saturated fat, 13.2g total protein, 68mg calcium, 0.71g sodium

Braised stuffed squid with spinach

I like the ingredients in this dish. Being a Thai person, I was born loving squid! Spinach is also a favourite of my son, Tim, so I tend to use it quite a lot when cooking for him. I'm lucky that I have no problem getting Tim to eat green vegetables! **Serves 4**

600g (1¼lb) potatoes, peeled and cut into slices 1cm (½in) thick
450g (1lb) spinach, large stalks removed and leaves washed
2 tablespoons olive oil
Salt and pepper
8 medium squid tubes, cleaned
65g (2½oz) vegan margarine, cut into small pieces
Hot chilli powder, to taste
Juice of 2 lemons
Parsley, to garnish

Cook the potatoes in a saucepan of boiling water for 10 minutes or until tender. Drain well and set aside.
Steam the spinach until very tender. Then drain well and leave to cool a little. Squeeze the excess water from the steamed spinach with your hands. Put the spinach in a bowl, add the olive oil, mix well and season with salt and pepper to your liking. Set aside.
Preheat the oven to 180°C/350°F/gas mark 4 and lightly oil a 2-litre (3½-pint) round casserole.
Spoon the spinach loosely into the squid pouches and seal the open end of each pouch with a wooden cocktail stick. Set aside.
Arrange the potato slices, slightly overlapping, on the bottom of the casserole. Scatter half of the margarine over the potato slices. Arrange the stuffed squid tubes on top of the potato and scatter the remainder of the margarine over the squid. Sprinkle with the hot chilli powder to taste and more salt and pepper. Cover the casserole and cook in the oven for about 35–40 minutes until the squid are tender.
When ready to serve, squeeze the juice from the lemons all over the squid and garnish with parsley.

Per serving: 415 kcals, 22.2g fat, 3.8g saturated fat, 25.8g total protein, 222mg calcium, 0.54g sodium

Grilled sea bream topped with ginger and fermented soya bean sauce

I used to make this dish with pomfret but my western customers found it too bony. Since I substituted the pomfret with sea bream, I have had no complaints! **Serves 4**

- 2 tablespoons tapioca flour
- 65ml (2½fl oz) water
- 2 sea bream, 750g (1lb 10oz) each, trimmed and gutted
- 2½ tablespoons vegetable oil
- 15cm (6in) piece of fresh root ginger, peeled and finely sliced lengthways
- 4 garlic cloves, crushed
- 2 tablespoons fermented soya beans
- 1 tablespoon light soy sauce
- 2 teaspoons Thai fish sauce
- 1½ tablespoons sugar
- 80g (3oz) dried straw mushrooms, soaked in warm water until soft, drained and squeezed dry
- 175g (6oz) oyster mushrooms, trimmed
- 4 spring onions, cut into 2.5cm (1in) lengths
- 850ml (1½ pints) chicken stock or water
- 1 tablespoon sesame oil

To garnish

- A few coriander leaves
- Ground white pepper

Put the tapioca flour in a small bowl and stir in the water to make a thin paste, then set aside.

Make 3 slashes, about 3mm (⅛in) deep, on each side of the sea bream, rub about 1 tablespoon of the oil all over the fish and put them on a baking tray.

Preheat the grill to medium and grill the fish for about 5–7 minutes on each side or until cooked. Keep warm.

Heat the remaining oil in a wok over a medium heat. Add the ginger, garlic and fermented soya beans and stir-fry for about 30 seconds. Stir in the soy sauce, fish sauce and sugar. Add all the mushrooms, spring onions and chicken stock or water and stir together. Add the tapioca flour mixture and stir for about 30 seconds until the sauce thickens to a consistency that is slightly thinner than gravy. Finally, stir in the sesame oil.

Remove the fish carefully from the bone and place on individual serving plates. Spoon the sauce and vegetables over and garnish with coriander leaves and a sprinkling of pepper.

Per serving: 375 kcals, 15.1g fat, 2.1g saturated fat, 32.2g total protein, 2g soya protein, 134mg calcium, 1.21g sodium

Fish pie

You can use any fish of your choice for this and you can also add some shellfish if you fancy. I have used haddock, cod and salmon because they are all quite flaky and the colour of the salmon is extremely appealing. To me, cooking is not just about the food tasting good – it has to look appetising too. **Serves 4**

- 1kg (2¼lb) potatoes, peeled, washed and cubed
- 500ml (18fl oz) soya milk
- 375g (13oz) mixed haddock, cod and salmon fillets
- 50g (2oz) vegan margarine
- 40g (1½oz) plain flour
- Salt and pepper
- 150g (5oz) frozen peas
- 20g (¾oz) chives, snipped
- 1 teaspoon chopped tarragon
- 2 tablespoons chopped parsley

Cook the potatoes in a large pan of boiling salted water for 20 minutes until tender.

Meanwhile, pour the soya milk into another saucepan and add the fish. Gently bring to the boil, then remove from the heat and leave to stand for about 5 minutes. Carefully lift out the fish, using a slotted spoon, place it on a plate and set aside. Measure approximately 200ml (7fl oz) of the soya milk and reserve it for the mash; keep the rest for the sauce.

To make the sauce, melt half the margarine in a heavy-based pan, and stir in the flour and cook for a minute. Slowly whisk in the remaining unmeasured soya milk to make the sauce and bring to the boil. Stir and simmer for a few minutes.

Preheat the oven to 200°C/400°F/gas mark 6.

Drain the potatoes and mash them well. Stir in the reserved soya milk and remaining margarine, and season with salt and pepper to your liking.

Add the peas to the sauce and heat gently for a couple of minutes without boiling. Stir in the chives and tarragon and immediately pour into a deep ovenproof dish. Flake in the fish, discarding any skin, and mix gently.

Spoon the mash over the top to cover the filling and use a fork to rough up the surface. Place the dish on a baking sheet and bake in the oven for 30–35 minutes until the mash is golden brown on top. Serve sprinkled with the parsley.

Per serving: 505 kcals, 17.9g fat, 3.5g saturated fat, 34.3g total protein, 3.8g soya protein, 83mg calcium, 0.32g sodium

Roast red snapper with chestnuts, raisins and apple chunks

Red snapper is quite popular in the States, and I have started to use it more in my cooking as it really is delicious. Baking a fish whole is a great way to keep it moist and succulent. **Serves 4**

- 1 red snapper, weighing about 1.5kg (3lb 5oz), or 2 smaller ones, cleaned
- Salt and pepper
- 2 tablespoons olive oil

For the sauce

- 3 tablespoons olive oil
- 1 onion, chopped
- 200g (7oz) cooked chestnuts
- Handful of raisins
- 2 cooking apples, cored and cut into large chunks
- 2 red apples, cored and cut into large chunks
- Juice of 1 orange

Preheat the oven to 200°C/400°F/gas mark 6. Wash and pat dry the fish, then season with salt and pepper inside and out. Place in an oiled roasting tin and brush the skin with olive oil to keep it moist. Set aside while you make the sauce.

Heat the olive oil for the sauce in a pan and gently stir-fry the onion, chestnuts, raisins and apple chunks for a few minutes. Gradually add the orange juice and cook on a low heat for a further 2–3 minutes.

Spoon the sauce over and around the fish, then cover with foil and bake in the oven for about 30 minutes until the fish is cooked. To test if the fish is done, insert a knife into the thickest part and lift out a little of the flesh: if the flesh comes away easily from the bones and is opaque, the fish is cooked through.

Carefully fillet the fish, transfer to individual serving plates and spoon the sauce around. Serve hot.

Per serving: 506 kcals, 18.3g fat, 2.8g saturated fat, 46.1g total protein, 132mg calcium, 0.28g sodium

Steamed cod fillet with triple-flavour vegetables

This is a very healthy dish and, as its name indicates, is brimming with flavour. It's also very quick and easy to prepare. I really like the texture of cod when it is steamed. Serves 4

4 cod fillets, each weighing about 200g (7oz)
4 tablespoons vegetable stock or water

For the sauce

1½ tablespoons vegetable oil
25g (1oz) carrot, cut into thin sticks
40g (1½oz) baby corn
50g (2oz) onion, chopped
50g (2oz) pineapple, chopped
40g (1½oz) tomato, chopped
40g (1½oz) mixed peppers, deseeded and chopped
30g (1¼oz) cucumber, quartered, deseeded and cut into thin sticks
30g (1¼oz) oyster mushrooms
1 tablespoon vegetable stock or water
2½ tablespoons Thai fish sauce
2 tablespoons tomato ketchup
1 tablespoon sugar
1 tablespoon distilled malt vinegar

Preheat a steamer to cook the fish. Put the fish on a plate, add the vegetable stock or water and place in the steamer for about 15–20 minutes or until it is cooked.

To make the sauce, heat the oil in a wok or large frying pan over a medium heat. Add the carrot and baby corn and stir-fry for about 30 seconds, then add the onion, pineapple, tomato, peppers, cucumber and oyster mushrooms and stir-fry, constantly tossing and turning the ingredients.

Stir in the stock or water, season with the fish sauce, tomato ketchup, sugar and vinegar and continue stir-frying and tossing the ingredients until everything is hot and just tender. Do not overcook.

To serve, place the fish fillets on individual serving plates and top with the sauce.

Per serving: 247 kcals, 5.7g fat, 0.8g saturated fat, 38.9g total protein, 42mg calcium, 1g sodium

Pan-fried monkfish with lemon and caper sauce

This is very simple and has a very strong but clean taste. What can I say – it's very me! Perfect for an informal dinner party, this goes well with some crisp green salad leaves. Serves 4

3 tablespoons olive oil
1kg (2¼lb) monkfish tail, filleted, skinned and cut into 4 steaks
Ground black pepper
Mixed salad leaves, to serve

For the sauce

3 tablespoons olive oil
4 shallots, chopped
1 tablespoon small capers, rinsed
4 tinned anchovies in oil, drained and chopped
3 tablespoons dry white wine or water
3 tablespoons freshly squeezed lemon juice

Heat the oil in a large frying pan over medium heat and fry the monkfish steaks, using a spatula to press them against the pan. Once one side is slightly brown, turn the fish over and repeat, lowering the heat if necessary, until the fish steaks are cooked and brown on both sides. Remove from the pan and keep warm.

Heat the oil for the sauce over low heat and stir-fry the shallots until they release their fragrance, taking care not to burn them. Add the capers and anchovies and fry for 1 minute. Gradually pour in the wine or water and bring to the boil, then immediately remove from the heat and add the lemon juice.

Place the fish on individual serving plates and top with the sauce. Sprinkle with ground black pepper and serve with mixed salad leaves.

Per serving: 332 kcals, 17.8g fat, 2.7g saturated fat, 40.3g total protein, 35mg calcium, 0.26g sodium

Chicken with fresh peppercorns and flaked almonds

To roast dried chillies, simply toast in a dry frying pan for a couple of minutes over a low heat and keep tossing and turning them so they don't burn. When they release their aroma, they are ready. **Serves 4**

150g (5oz) plain flour
130ml (4½fl oz) water
200g (7oz) skinless, boneless chicken breast, thinly sliced
Vegetable oil, for deep-frying
2 garlic cloves, pounded with 2 fresh coriander roots to make a paste
7.5cm (3in) piece of fresh root ginger, peeled and finely cut into matchsticks
2 tablespoons Thai fish sauce
1½ tablespoons sugar
1 tablespoon fresh green peppercorns (see page 120)
30g (1¼oz) flaked almonds
2 spring onions, cut into 1.5cm (⅔in) lengths
2 roasted dried chillies, chopped
30g (1¼oz) carrot, cut into matchsticks
50g (2oz) mixed peppers, deseeded and sliced
A few coriander leaves, to garnish

Put 100g (3½oz) of the flour in a bowl and add the water to make a smooth paste.
Coat the chicken slices with the flour paste, then lift them up and let the excess paste drip off. Lightly sprinkle the slices with the remaining dry flour to hold the paste in place.
Heat enough oil for deep-frying in a wok over a high heat until it reaches 180°C/356°F. Deep-fry the chicken slices for about 2–3 minutes until they are crisp and float to the surface. Remove from the oil and drain on kitchen paper. Keep warm.
Heat 2 tablespoons of fresh vegetable oil in the wok over medium heat. Add the garlic, coriander paste and ginger and stir-fry for about 15 seconds, taking care not to burn them. Season with the fish sauce and sugar. Add a splash of water if necessary.
Stir in the peppercorns, almonds, spring onions, chillies, carrot and mixed peppers. Add the chicken and continue stir-frying, constantly turning, until heated through.
Transfer to a serving plate and garnish with coriander leaves.

Per serving: 510 kcals, 31.2g fat, 3.6g saturated fat, 19.1g total protein, 102mg calcium, 0.61g sodium

Baked poussins with lemon and oregano

I like using lemon juice in many dishes. It really makes ordinary food taste better. People say that lemon juice is good only with seafood and chicken, but if you know how to use it properly it will go with almost any type of meat. **Serves 4**

4 poussins
3 tablespoons plain flour
2 tablespoons olive oil
1½ tablespoons grated lemon zest
1 onion, finely chopped
2 oregano sprigs, leaves only, finely chopped
350ml (12fl oz) dry white wine
Salt and ground black pepper
Vegetables, to serve

Preheat the oven to 180°C/350°F/gas mark 4.
Pat the poussins dry with kitchen paper, then dust with the flour to coat lightly all over. Set aside.
Heat the oil in a large heavy-based pan over a medium heat. Stir in the lemon zest, onion and oregano and finally add the wine. Sauté until the onion turns tender and golden and the wine has half evaporated.
Place the poussins in a baking tray, pour half the sauce over them and season to taste with salt and pepper. Bake in the oven for 35 minutes, turning once. When turning, pour over the rest of the sauce to ensure that the poussins are not too dry.
Transfer the poussins to individual serving plates and spoon any sauce left in the baking tray over them. Serve with your preferred choice of vegetables, such as broccoli and carrots.

Per serving: 627 kcals, 38.1g fat, 9.8g saturated fat, 46g total protein, 52mg calcium, 0.26g sodium

Chicken and vegetables with cashew nuts and roasted dried chillies

In my restaurant, I serve either chicken with cashew nuts and roasted dried chillies or the veggie version. The following recipe is the combination of both. Serves 4

- 2 tablespoons vegetable oil
- 150g (5oz) skinless boneless chicken breast, thinly sliced
- 275g (10oz) mixed seasonal vegetables of your choice (such as baby corn, broccoli, carrots, French beans and mangetout), prepared
- 4 tablespoons vegetable stock or water
- 3 teaspoons sugar
- 1½ tablespoons Thai fish sauce
- Salt, to taste
- 1 teaspoon dark soy sauce
- ½ handful of cashew nuts, roasted
- 3 large roasted dried chillies (see page 114), cut into small pieces with a pair of scissors
- A few coriander leaves, to garnish
- Boiled rice (see page 49), to serve

Heat the oil in a wok over a medium heat. Add the chicken and stir-fry until almost cooked.

Add the vegetables to the wok, starting with the ones that need the longest cooking time, and stir-fry, tossing and turning until they are half cooked. Stir in the stock or water, then reduce the heat.

Season with the sugar, fish sauce, salt to taste and dark soy sauce, turn up the heat to high and continue stir-frying for a few seconds until all the vegetables are tender but still crisp. Stir in the cashew nuts and dried chillies.

Transfer the chicken and vegetables to a serving plate and garnish with the coriander leaves. This dish is great served with plain boiled rice.

Per serving: 165 kcals, 9.2g fat, 1.1g saturated fat, 12.6g total protein, 35mg calcium, 0.68g sodium

Roast chicken with sage and balsamic vinegar

I like strong tastes in my food and I find balsamic vinegar has great character. This western-style dish is so simple to make – you just need to remember to allow enough time for marinating the chicken to get the best flavour. Serves 4

- 50ml (2fl oz) extra virgin olive oil
- 2 tablespoons balsamic vinegar
- 1 tablespoon chopped sage
- 1 garlic clove, crushed
- Ground black pepper
- 2 baby chickens, weighing about 500g (18oz) each, cut in half, backbone removed and flattened
- Baked potatoes and dressed salad, to serve

Combine all the ingredients (except the chickens) to make a marinade. Place the chickens in a large dish and pour the marinade over them, rub in well and cover the dish. Leave to marinate for a couple of hours in the fridge.

Preheat the oven to 180°C/350°F/gas mark 4.

Place the marinated chicken halves on a roasting rack set over a tin and roast for about 40–45 minutes, basting every so often, until cooked. Serve with baked potatoes and salad leaves dressed with olive oil and balsamic vinegar.

Per serving: 402 kcals, 31.6g fat, 7.2g saturated fat, 27.9g total protein, 19mg calcium, 0.11g sodium

Holy basil pork liver

I'm quite anaemic and as liver is a good source of iron, my grandmother used to force me to eat a dish similar to this one. I hated it the first time but now I love it, especially when it is cooked with chilli and holy basil. It is so tasty! **Serves 4**

2 tablespoons vegetable oil
2 garlic cloves, pounded with 1 fresh red chilli to make a coarse paste
350g (12oz) pork liver, sliced into bite-size pieces
100g (3½oz) onion, sliced
2 tablespoons Thai fish sauce
1½ teaspoons sugar
½ teaspoon dark soy sauce
3 tablespoons chicken stock or water
2 fresh red chillies, sliced lengthways
½ handful of holy basil leaves
Boiled rice (see page 49), to serve

Heat the oil in a wok or a frying pan over a medium heat. Add the garlic and chilli paste and stir around for 10 seconds, taking care not to burn it.

Add the pork liver pieces and onion and continue stir-frying, constantly tossing and turning, for a few minutes. Season with the fish sauce, sugar and soy sauce and continue stirring to blend all the seasoning. Add the stock or water, followed by the chillies and holy basil leaves and stir-fry for a further 15 seconds.

Serve immediately with plain boiled rice.

Per serving: 176 kcals, 8.3g fat, 1.5g saturated fat, 20.4g total protein, 25mg calcium, 0.71g sodium

Roast pork with rosemary

A very easy dish as the pork makes its own tasty gravy as it cooks. Serve with a selection of boiled or steamed seasonal vegetables and if you like, apple sauce on the side – the traditional western accompaniment. **Serves 5**

1 boned and rolled loin of pork, about 1kg (2¼lb)
Salt and coarsely ground black pepper
2 tablespoons olive oil
1 celery stick, chopped
1 onion, chopped
1 garlic clove, crushed
2 tablespoons chopped rosemary, plus 2 whole rosemary sprigs
150ml (¼ pint) dry white wine
250ml (9fl oz) vegetable stock

Preheat the oven to 180°C/350°F/gas mark 4.

Rub the pork loin with salt and black pepper. Heat the olive oil in a flameproof casserole, add the pork and brown well on all sides. Lift the pork out and set aside on a large plate.

Add the vegetables, garlic and chopped rosemary to the casserole and season with salt to taste. Sauté for 5 minutes and place the meat on top. Turn up the heat, pour in the wine and let it bubble rapidly for a minute, turning the pork over once. Then add half of the vegetable stock.

Cover the casserole and cook in the oven for 1½ hours or until the pork is tender, turning the joint twice. If the vegetables seem to be drying out, add a little more stock. Lay the rosemary sprigs on top of the pork about 25 minutes before the end of the cooking time.

To serve, remove the rind from the pork and carve the meat into slices, then pour the sauce over it.

Per serving: 424 kcals, 27.3g fat, 9.4g saturated fat, 37g total protein, 48mg calcium, 0.23g sodium

Roast duck red curry with pineapple and seedless grapes

In Thailand, the only curry we make using precooked meat is roast duck curry, because we find that duck smells too strong to use in any of our cooking unless it is first roasted with spices. **Serves 4**

5 kaffir lime leaves, torn
4 tablespoons ready-made Thai red curry paste
1 tablespoon vegetable oil
250ml (8fl oz) coconut milk
250ml (8fl oz) soya milk
250g (9oz) roast duck fillets, sliced (skin removed)
½ handful of pineapple slices (if using tinned, save the juice or syrup and use it instead of water, reducing the amount of sugar used accordingly)
20g (¾oz) frozen peas
8 baby tomatoes
½ handful of seedless grapes
200ml (7fl oz) water
4 tablespoons Thai fish sauce
1½ tablespoons sugar
Boiled rice (see page 49), to serve

To garnish
1 fresh green chilli, sliced lengthways
10–12 sweet basil leaves

Stir-fry the kaffir lime leaves and red curry paste with the oil in a wok or a saucepan, for about a minute, taking care not to burn the curry paste. Gently add the coconut and soya milk, stirring well, and let it simmer on a low heat for about 5–7 minutes or until oil starts to appear on the surface.

Add the roast duck, pineapple slices, peas, tomatoes and grapes together with the water, or juice from the pineapple (see above) and bring the curry to the boil. Lower the heat and season with the fish sauce and sugar. Give it one good stir, making sure the curry sauce covers all the ingredients, and simmer for 1 minute.

Garnish with the sliced chillies and sweet basil leaves and serve hot with plain boiled rice.

Per serving: 337 kcals, 23g fat, 10.7g saturated fat, 19.9g total protein, 1.7g soya protein, 163mg calcium, 1.59g sodium

Spare ribs with ginger sauce

I have been living abroad for more than half of my life and I don't often see spare ribs on the menus of western restaurants, except in some American grills. I like barbecue spare ribs, western-style, but I think you can do more with them and here is an example. **Serves 4**

850g (1lb 14oz) spare ribs, cut into 5cm (2in) lengths
2 tablespoons vegetable oil
2 teaspoons fermented soya beans
1–2 tablespoons water
8 dried jelly mushrooms (ear mushrooms), soaked in warm water until soft, drained and squeezed dry
80g (3oz) onion, sliced
2 tablespoons Thai fish sauce
1½ tablespoons sugar
1 tablespoon distilled malt vinegar
1 teaspoon dark soy sauce
6cm (2½in) piece of fresh root ginger, peeled and finely sliced lengthways
4 spring onions, cut into 5cm (2in) lengths
Ground white pepper
1 fresh red chilli, thinly sliced
A few coriander leaves

Cook the spare ribs in boiling water for about 5 minutes, then lower the heat to medium and continue to cook for another 10–15 minutes until the meat is tender and easily slides off the bone. Drain well and set aside.

Heat the oil over a medium heat in a frying pan or a wok, add the fermented soya beans and stir around for about 10 seconds, taking care not to burn them. Add the cooked spare ribs and stir-fry, constantly tossing and turning, for about 1–2 minutes until the spare ribs absorb some of the sauce.

Add 1 tablespoon of water to keep the spare ribs moist and stir in the jelly mushrooms and onion. Season with the fish sauce, sugar, vinegar and soy sauce. Add the ginger and spring onions and continue stir-frying for about 15 seconds, when the dish should be ready. If it seems too dry, just add a little more water.

Transfer all the ingredients to a serving plate, sprinkle with ground white pepper and garnish with red chilli slices and coriander leaves. Serve with plain boiled rice.

Per serving: 306 kcals, 19.4g fat, 5.5g saturated fat, 21.4g total protein, 2g soya protein, 43mg calcium, 0.86g sodium

Yellow curry with lamb and onions

This dish is influenced by Thailand's neighbour countries, such as Malaysia and Indonesia, together with the Thai population living in and around the south of Thailand where there is a huge Muslim population. **Serves 4**

- 310g (11oz) lamb fillet, cubed
- 1 tablespoon vegetable oil
- 4 tablespoons ready-made yellow curry paste
- 200ml (7fl oz) coconut milk
- 200ml (7fl oz) soya milk
- 200ml (7fl oz) water
- 4 potatoes, peeled and cut into chunks
- 1 large carrot, cut into chunks
- 1 large onion, quartered
- 2 tablespoons Thai fish sauce
- 1 tablespoon sugar
- 6 cardamom leaves
- Salt and pepper
- Naan bread, pitta bread or boiled rice (see page 49), to serve

Put the lamb in a saucepan, cover with water, bring to the boil and simmer on a medium heat until the meat is tender. Put the potato chunks in boiling water and cook for 10 minutes until par-boiled, then drain and set aside.

Heat the oil in another saucepan and stir-fry the yellow curry paste for a minute, taking care not to burn it. Add the coconut and soya milk and bring to the boil. Drain the lamb cubes well and add to the curry sauce. Add the measured water, potatoes, carrot and onion and return to the boil. Turn down the heat to low and simmer for about 10 minutes to let the sauce penetrate the lamb.

Season with the fish sauce, sugar and cardamom leaves and continue to simmer until the potatoes are soft and tender. Adjust the seasoning to taste and remove from the heat.

Serve hot with warm naan bread, pitta bread or boiled rice.

Per serving: 434 kcals, 26g fat, 12.8g saturated fat, 21.6g total protein, 1.5g soya protein, 151mg calcium, 0.94g sodium

Grilled lamb chops with fresh peppercorns, coriander root and shallots

If you cannot find fresh peppercorns then buy preserved peppercorns in brine, oil or vinegar, and wash thoroughly before using. They will have the right soft texture. **Serves 4**

- 1 tablespoon fresh green peppercorns
- 1 tablespoon chopped fresh coriander root
- 1 tablespoon olive oil
- Sea salt and ground black pepper
- 4 lamb chops (trimmed of fat)
- 450g (1lb) shallots, unpeeled
- 3 large potatoes, quartered
- 100ml (3½fl oz) beef stock
- 30g (1¼oz) vegan margarine

Preheat the oven to 180°C/350°F/gas mark 4.

To make a marinade, in a large bowl mix together half of the green peppercorns, half of the chopped coriander root and the olive oil with salt and pepper to taste. Add the lamb chops and rub the marinade all over each one to make sure they are well coated. Cover and leave to marinate in the fridge for 20 minutes.

Meanwhile, place the shallots and potatoes in a roasting tin and bake in the oven for 45 minutes. Remove from the oven and allow to cool. Top and tail the shallots using a small knife and squeeze them out of their skins. Set aside with the potatoes.

Heat a lightly oiled griddle pan or preheat the grill to its highest setting and griddle or grill the marinated lamb chops for 3–4 minutes on each side or to your liking.

While the chops are cooking, put the remainder of the green peppercorns with the cooked shallots and potatoes in a saucepan, add the beef stock and place over a high heat until the stock has almost completely evaporated. Reduce the heat to medium and add the margarine together with the remainder of the chopped coriander root. Season with salt and pepper and stir until the margarine has melted.

Serve the grilled lamb chops with the vegetable mixture.

Per serving: 407 kcals, 19g fat, 9.3g saturated fat, 33.6g total protein, 71mg calcium, 0.28g sodium

Beef stroganoff

When I was studying in the States, my guardian, uncle Don, an American friend of my dad, used to make this dish for us every week. I loved it, and I've devised this recipe that replaces the usual soured dairy cream with soya cream so that non-dairy eaters can enjoy it too. **Serves 4**

350g (12oz) rump steak, cut into thick strips
Salt and ground black pepper
75g (3oz) vegan margarine
1 large onion, halved and thinly sliced
225g (8oz) button mushrooms
4 tablespoons brandy
100ml (3½fl oz) beef or chicken stock
75ml (3fl oz) soya cream
75ml (3fl oz) soya milk
30ml (1¼oz) grainy mustard
1 tablespoon chopped tarragon
1 tablespoon snipped chives
Boiled rice (see page 49) or pasta, to serve

Toss the steak strips in black pepper. Heat 50g (2oz) of the margarine in a heavy-based frying pan until hot and sizzling. Cook the steak strips, in batches, for a couple of minutes. Remove from the pan and keep warm.

Heat the remaining margarine in the pan and cook the onion and mushrooms for a few minutes. Add the brandy, stock and soya cream and soya milk, and leave simmering until the sauce thickens. Stir in the mustard and tarragon and season with salt and black pepper.

Put the beef into the sauce and heat, stirring, until the meat is hot. Sprinkle with the snipped chives and serve with boiled rice or pasta.

Per serving: 389 kcals, 28.9g fat, 7.6g saturated fat, 21.6g total protein, 0.5g soya protein, 79mg calcium, 0.47g sodium

Spicy linguine with minced beef and basil

The Italians use so many similar herbs and ingredients to the Thais in their cooking and this dish is one very good example. It reminds me of a spaghetti Bolognese but spicier and without tomatoes. A winning formula! **Serves 2–3**

350g (12oz) dried linguine
Salt and pepper

For the sauce

2 tablespoons extra virgin olive oil
1 garlic clove, pounded with 1 fresh red chilli to make a coarse paste
200g (7oz) minced lean beef
80g (3oz) onion, finely chopped
1½ tablespoons Thai fish sauce
1 tablespoon sugar
½ teaspoon dark soy sauce
2½ tablespoons water
1 fresh chilli, sliced lengthways
10 holy basil leaves

Cook the linguine in a large pan of boiling salted water, according to the packet instructions, until tender but firm to the bite.

Meanwhile, make the sauce. Heat the oil in a frying pan over a medium heat. Add the garlic and chilli paste and stir around for 10 seconds. Add the beef and continue stir-frying, constantly tossing and turning, for about 2 minutes until it is half cooked.

Add the onion and stir-fry for a further 20 seconds, then season with the fish sauce, sugar and soy sauce and continue stirring. Add the water, then stir in most of the chilli and most of the holy basil leaves and stir-fry for another 15–20 seconds.

Add the cooked drained pasta to the sauce and mix in well. Transfer the pasta with the sauce to individual serving plates. Garnish with the remaining chilli and holy basil.

Per serving (for 3): 628 kcals, 15.9g fat, 4.1g saturated fat, 30.2g total protein, 53mg calcium, 0.84g sodium

Beef hotpot with onions and Yorkshire puddings

This is a very cosy and homely type of dish. Since my boarding-school years I have always loved Yorkshire pudding with gravy. And these soya milk versions taste just the same as regular ones! **Serves 4**

500g (18oz) stewing beef, cubed
750ml (26fl oz) beef stock
2 thyme sprigs
Salt and ground black pepper
400g (14oz) large onions, quartered
1½ tablespoons brown sugar
2 tablespoons plain flour
400g (14oz) small baking potatoes, peeled
400g (14oz) carrots, cut into chunks

Put the beef in a heavy-based pan with the stock and thyme sprigs. Season with salt and pepper and bring to the boil. Lower the heat and simmer for 30 minutes.

Add the onions to the pan, stir in the sugar and simmer for another 20 minutes.

Meanwhile, preheat the oven to 180°C/350°F/gas mark 4.

Mix the flour with a little water to make a runny paste, pour into the pan and stir in well to thicken. Transfer the contents of the pan to an ovenproof dish, stir in the potatoes and carrots and cover with the lid. Cook in the oven for at least 1 hour until the beef is tender. Remove from the oven and keep warm while you cook the Yorkshire puddings.

Per serving (without Yorkshire puddings): 382 kcals, 8.9g fat, 3.5g saturated fat, 33.2g total protein, 104mg calcium, 0.46g sodium

Yorkshire puddings

80g (3oz) plain flour
Salt and pepper
1 medium egg, beaten
125ml (4fl oz) soya milk
2–3 tablespoons olive oil

Raise the temperature of the oven to 220°C/425°F/gas mark 7. Put the flour in a mixing bowl, and add a pinch of salt and pepper. Add the beaten egg in the middle of the flour and slowly whisk in the soya milk, working from the centre outwards, until all the flour is incorporated.

Put some oil into each section of an 8-hole Yorkshire pudding tin and place it in the oven for about 5 minutes until the oil is very hot and sizzling. Divide the batter between the sections of the tin and bake in the oven for 15–20 minutes until well risen and crisp on top.

Serve with the beef, vegetables and gravy.

Per serving (Yorkshire puddings only): 145 kcals, 7.7g fat, 1.2g saturated fat, 4.2g total protein, 1g soya protein, 40mg calcium, 0.12g sodium

5 Desserts and Drinks

Oriental fruit salad

This is extremely refreshing and a wonderful dessert to follow a spicy and heavy main course. It is also lovely to have with crushed ice on a hot summer's day. If fresh jackfruit and palm fruit are unavailable, substitute tinned, but discard the syrup. Serves 4

600ml (1 pint) orange juice
2 tablespoons caster sugar
1 tablespoon freshly squeezed lime juice
1 ripe but firm mango, peeled and cut into small cubes
1 ripe but firm papaya, peeled and cut into small cubes
4 pieces of jackfruit, torn into strips
4 palm fruits, cut into strips
¼ small pineapple, peeled, cored and cut into bite-size pieces

Put the orange juice in a jug and stir in the caster sugar. Add the lime juice and stir well. Set aside.
Place all the fruits in a large glass bowl. Pour in the prepared juice, cover with clingfilm and refrigerate.
Serve chilled, by itself or with any fruit sorbet.

Per serving: 239 kcals, 0.6g fat, 0g saturated fat, 2.8g total protein, 66mg calcium, 0.02g sodium

Crispy fresh mango with cinnamon and berry sauce

My alternative to the banana fritters usually served in Oriental restaurants. The chilled berry sauce goes extremely well with the warm crispy mango slices. It's certainly a hit with the customers at my restaurant. Serves 4

Vegetable oil, for deep-frying
2 ripe but firm mangoes, peeled and sliced lengthways into strips 1cm (½in) wide
110g (4oz) plain flour

For the sauce
150g (5oz) mixed berries (such as raspberries, blueberries and strawberries)
1½ tablespoons caster sugar
100ml (3fl oz) cranberry juice
Juice of 1 lime

To garnish
½ handful of mixed berries
4 mint sprigs
Ground cinnamon

First make the sauce by putting all the ingredients in a blender and blending until smooth. Refrigerate.
Heat enough oil for deep-frying in a wok to 180°C/356°F. Lightly coat the mango strips with the flour and slide them one by one into the hot oil. Fry until they are lightly browned and crisp, gently turning them over once or twice to make sure they are cooked evenly on both sides.
Remove from the hot oil using a wire spoon or a pair of tongs and drain well on kitchen paper.
Arrange the crispy fried mango slices on serving plates. Garnish each plate with berries and a sprig of mint and sprinkle them with ground cinnamon. Serve the chilled berry sauce in a separate bowl.

Per serving: 365 kcals, 15.8g fat, 1.8g saturated fat, 4.1g total protein, 82mg calcium, 0.01g sodium

Pan-fried fresh pineapple and toasted coconut

Instead of the usual banana in caramel sauce, why not try this caramelised pineapple? You can adapt this recipe by drizzling the pan-fried pineapple with runny honey instead of brown sugar, if you wish. Serves 4

- 1 tablespoon desiccated coconut
- 1 medium pineapple, peeled, cored and halved lengthways
- 30g (1¼oz) vegan margarine
- 4 tablespoons light brown sugar
- 4 tablespoons freshly squeezed lime juice
- Lime wedges, to decorate
- Dairy-free coconut or vanilla ice cream, to serve

Dry-fry the desiccated coconut in a frying pan over a very low heat, constantly stirring to prevent burning, until it is lightly browned. Set aside.

Cut the pineapple flesh lengthways into 1–1.5cm (½–⅔in) wedges and set aside.

Meanwhile, heat half of the vegan margarine in a large frying pan over a low heat. Slide about 4 of the pineapple wedges into the pan and cook on each side for a few minutes or until they turn slightly golden.

Sprinkle half of the sugar evenly all over the pineapple wedges followed by half of the lime juice. Continue to stir constantly to make sure the sugar melts. Turn over the pineapple wedges once. Remove from the pan and keep warm while you fry the remaining pineapple wedges in the same way.

Transfer the caramelised pineapple to a large serving plate and sprinkle with the toasted coconut. Decorate with lime wedges and serve with dairy-free coconut or vanilla ice cream.

Per serving (without ice cream): 205 kcals, 8.4g fat, 2.9g saturated fat, 1g total protein, 45mg calcium, 0.06g sodium

Peaches with meringue and chopped almonds

Peaches are one of my favourite fruits – they are juicy and succulent. This dessert is very light yet satisfying, with so many blends of different flavours and textures. Serves 4

- 30g (1¼oz) vegan margarine
- 4 large peaches, halved
- 1 tablespoon chopped almonds
- 1 egg white
- 40g (1½oz) golden caster sugar

Preheat the oven to 200°C/400°F/gas mark 6. In the oven, melt the margarine in a small roasting tin, then place the peach halves in the tin and scatter in the almonds. Roast for 20 minutes, turning from time to time until the peaches are tender.

Meanwhile, whisk the egg white in a mixing bowl to stiff peaks, then gradually whisk in the sugar to make a firm and glossy meringue.

Turn the peaches cut side up in the roasting tin and spoon some meringue on top of each one. Return to the oven for a further 5 minutes or until the meringue is lightly browned.

Serve the meringue-topped peaches hot, with their juice and the nuts from the roasting tin.

Per serving: 170 kcals, 8.4g fat, 1.4g saturated fat, 3.2g total protein, 26mg calcium, 0.08g sodium

Baked apples with walnuts and custard

When one of my restaurant staff was returning to Thailand for good, I organised a farewell party for her and she begged me to make western dishes. This apple dessert was one of the dishes I knocked up. Serves 4

2 Granny Smith apples, cored but not peeled
2 Red Delicious apples, cored but not peeled
30g (1¼oz) walnut pieces
30g (1¼oz) sultanas
2 tablespoons brown sugar
2 tablespoons runny honey
20g (¾oz) vegan margarine, plus extra for greasing

For the custard
285ml (9½fl oz) soya milk
½ tablespoon custard powder
1 egg yolk
½ teaspoon vanilla essence
Sugar, to taste

Preheat the oven to 190°C/375°F/gas mark 5. Grease a baking tin large enough to hold all 4 apples.
Enlarge the core opening at the stem end of each apple to about 2.5cm (1in) in diameter by cutting at an angle with a small knife. Arrange the apples stem-end up in the prepared tin. Fill them with a mixture of walnut pieces and sultanas, sprinkle with brown sugar and drizzle with honey. Top each with a quarter of the margarine and bake in the oven for 45 minutes.
Meanwhile, make the custard. Warm most of the soya milk in a saucepan over a medium heat (reserve 1 tablespoon) but do not let it boil. In a bowl, mix the custard powder with the reserved soya milk until smooth. Blend in the egg yolk and vanilla essence and pour the warm soya milk over the custard mixture, whisking constantly. Return the mixture to the saucepan and stir over a low heat until it thickens. Sweeten with sugar to taste.
Serve the apples hot with the soya milk custard.

Per serving: 287 kcals, 12.2g fat, 2g saturated fat, 4.4g total protein, 2g soya protein, 39mg calcium, 0.07g sodium

Pear crumble

You can make a scrumptious dairy-free crumble topping for this classic western dessert, and the fruit is precooked using vegan margarine to give it a luxurious texture. It is delicious with dairy-free custard (see the recipe to the left). Serves 4

25g (1oz) vegan margarine
6 ripe but firm pears, peeled, cored and chopped
50g (2oz) caster sugar
Dairy-free custard (see left), to serve

For the crumble topping
80g (3oz) vegan margarine
110g (4oz) caster sugar
165g (5½oz) plain flour

Preheat the oven to 180°C/350°F/gas mark 4.
Melt the margarine in a pan, add the chopped pears and cook over a high heat, constantly stirring and turning, until the fruit is soft and most of the liquid has evaporated.
Add the sugar and stir in well to make sure it is completely dissolved. Remove from the heat and transfer the fruit and syrup to a baking dish.
To make the topping, put all the ingredients in a bowl and rub them between your fingers until the mixture resembles breadcrumbs.
Spread the crumble mixture evenly over the pears and bake for 25–30 minutes or until the top is golden brown.
Serve the pear crumble hot with custard.

Per serving: 581 kcals, 22.2g fat, 4.5g saturated fat, 4.6g total protein, 2g soya protein, 88mg calcium, 0.22g sodium

Black sticky rice pudding with young coconut flesh

Most Thai puddings and desserts use coconut milk or cream as a main ingredient where western desserts would use dairy products. This makes a great alternative to the traditional rice pudding. Serves 4

¼ teaspoon salt
75ml (3fl oz) coconut cream
275g (10oz) black sticky rice
600ml (1 pint) water
225g (8oz) sugar
125g (4oz) young coconut flesh, cut into strips

Mix the salt and coconut cream together in a pan over a very low heat, stirring constantly to prevent the cream from separating. Remove from the heat as soon as the salt has dissolved and set aside.

Wash the rice twice, place in a pan and add the water. Place over a medium heat and boil until the rice is cooked through. The grains will split when they are cooked. Add the sugar and continue to boil and gently stir until it has totally dissolved.

Spoon the sticky rice pudding into individual serving bowls and top each portion with a few coconut strips and a spoonful of the coconut cream. When ready to eat, stir both the coconut strips and the coconut cream into the pudding.

Per serving: 546 kcals, 9.2g fat, 6.7g saturated fat, 6.9g total protein, 15mg calcium, 0.16g sodium

Bananas in coconut milk with sweetcorn kernels

A very comforting pudding – you'll love the creamy coconut sauce. Pandanus leaves are available from Thai supermarkets but if you can't find one, simply omit, as the toasted sesame seeds provide plenty of flavour. Serves 4

2 teaspoons sesame seeds
400ml (14fl oz) coconut milk
200ml (7fl oz) water
1 pandanus leaf, cleaned, wiped dry and tied into a knot (optional)
100g (3½oz) sugar
½ teaspoon salt
4 tablespoons fresh or drained tinned sweetcorn kernels
4 ripe but firm medium bananas, peeled, halved lengthways and each half cut into 6–8 pieces

Dry-fry the sesame seeds in a frying pan over a low heat until they release their aroma and turn golden brown. Set aside.

Put the coconut milk and water in a saucepan over medium heat and bring to the boil. Add the knotted pandanus leaf (if using) and simmer for a few minutes. Stir in the sugar and salt. If using fresh sweetcorn, add it now and cook for a further minute or so.

Add the banana pieces and, if you are using it, the tinned sweetcorn and simmer for about 1½ minutes until the banana pieces are tender but not too soft. Discard the pandanus leaf.

Spoon the bananas and coconut milk into individual serving bowls. Sprinkle with the toasted sesame seeds and serve warm.

Per serving: 383 kcals, 18.2g fat, 14.3g saturated fat, 3.6g total protein, 55mg calcium, 0.35g sodium

Coconut crème caramels

Another traditional western dessert which has been given a new twist with dairy-free ingredients. Here, coconut milk replaces the usual cow's milk with superb results. This also makes a fabulous dinner party dessert. Serves 6

165g (5½oz) caster sugar
400ml (14fl oz) coconut milk
3 eggs
A few drops of vanilla essence

Preheat the oven to 150°C/300°F/gas mark 2.
Put 65g (2½oz) of the sugar in a heavy-based pan over a low heat. Stir until the sugar has melted and then continue heating until it turns golden brown, watching it like a hawk so that it does not burn. Quickly pour equal amounts of the caramelised sugar into 4 ramekins and place them in a roasting tin.
Heat the coconut milk in a saucepan over a low heat until warm but do not boil. Beat the eggs in a bowl with the remaining sugar until the texture is light and creamy. Gradually add the warm coconut milk, constantly beating the mixture, and then add the vanilla.
Strain the custard mixture into a jug and pour an aqual amount into each ramekin. Carefully pour hot water into the roasting tin to come half way up the outside of the ramekins. Place the tin in the oven and bake for 35-40 minutes, until the custards are set. Leave to cool and refrigerate.
When ready to eat, run a knife around the edge of each ramekin and invert on to individual serving plates.

Per serving: 262 kcals, 14.2g fat, 10.2g saturated fat, 4.7g total protein, 39mg calcium, 0.17g sodium

Lemon cheesecake with strawberries

I actually prefer this cheesecake to the usual dairy-laden recipe. It tastes much lighter and fresher. Thanks to my friend Noi who helped me with this recipe at the expense of her husband's birthday cake! Serves 6

50g (2oz) vegan margarine
50g (2oz) caster sugar
175g (6oz) digestive biscuits, crushed
3 tablespoons dairy-free lemon curd
Fresh strawberries, to decorate

For the filling
Juice and grated zest of 1 lemon
4 tablespoons water
1 tablespoon gelatine, or a vegetarian alternative such as agar or carrageen
225g (8oz) vegan quark or other dairy-free soft cheese
150ml (¼ pint) soya milk
80g (3oz) caster sugar

Melt the vegan margarine and sugar over a gentle heat. Stir in the crushed biscuits and mix well. Press into the base of a 20cm (8in) round springform cake tin in an even layer and chill in the fridge.
To make the filling, put the lemon juice and zest, water and gelatine in a bowl resting over a pan of hot water and stir until the gelatine has dissolved. Leave to cool. Soften the quark in a large mixing bowl, mix in the soya milk and sugar and beat until blended. Add the gelatine mixture and stir well. Spoon on to the biscuit base and chill for 3-4 hours until set.
Remove the cheesecake from the tin and place on a serving plate. Spread the top with the lemon curd and decorate with fresh strawberries.

Per serving: 349 kcals, 13.7g fat, 3.3g saturated fat, 9.6g total protein, 0.6g soya protein, 107mg calcium, 0.24g sodium

Chocolate brownies with banana and chunky chestnuts

This is my trademark dessert at my restaurant. Cooked chestnuts are quite expensive, but I recommend that you buy good-quality ones which are firm and chunky, rather than the cheaper flaky and soft ones. Serves 8–12

175g (6oz) luxury dark chocolate (at least 75 per cent cocoa)
175g (6oz) vegan margarine, plus extra for greasing
2 very ripe medium bananas, peeled
2 medium eggs
120g (4¼oz) plain flour
½ teaspoon baking powder
120g (4¼oz) caster sugar
½ teaspoon salt
200g (7oz) jar or vacuum-packed cooked whole chestnuts

for the chocolate sauce

100g (3½oz) luxury dark chocolate (at least 75 per cent cocoa)
25g (1oz) vegan margarine

Preheat the oven to 175°C/325°F/gas mark 3.
Break up the chocolate into a heatproof bowl and add the margarine. Set over a pan of gently simmering water and melt, stirring occasionally. (You will also use this method to make the chocolate sauce; see below.)
Mash the bananas in a large mixing bowl. Beat the eggs into the bananas until the whites and yolks are well blended. Add the flour, baking powder, sugar and salt, then immediately add the warm chocolate mixture and gently fold in.
Add most of the chestnuts to the mixture and gently fold in. Pour the mixture into a greased non-stick rectangular cake tin, 18cm (7in) x 25cm (10in) x 2.5cm (1in) deep, and ensure that the chestnuts are evenly distributed. Use the reserved chestnuts to fill any gaps and make sure that all the chestnuts are covered with the mixture. Bake on the middle shelf of the oven for 25–30 minutes until the mixture is set.
Leave to cool in the tin for 10–15 minutes before cutting into squares for serving.
To make the chocolate sauce, follow the method above.
Serve the brownies with the hot chocolate sauce.

Per serving (for 12): 383 kcals, 24.5g fat, 7.9g saturated fat, 4.3g total protein, 40mg calcium, 0.25g sodium

Coffee gateau

I am most grateful to my friend Noi for supplying me with this recipe. She makes cakes for a living and she created this gateau at my request. It works beautifully and is so decadent – it is definitely a very grown-up kind of cake!
Serves 6–8

110g (4oz) self-raising flour
2 teaspoons baking powder
Pinch of salt
110g (4oz) caster sugar
4 large eggs, separated
180ml (6½fl oz) groundnut oil
180ml (6½fl oz) water
1 teaspoon coffee essence
½ teaspoon cream of tartar

For the coffee cream icing

110g (4oz) vegan margarine
175g (6oz) icing sugar
1 teaspoon instant coffee powder, mixed with 1 teaspoon hot water and left to cool
Pinch of instant coffee powder, to decorate.

Preheat the oven to 170°C/325°F/gas mark 3.
Mix together the flour, baking powder, salt and half of the sugar in a large bowl, and make a well in the centre. Mix the egg yolks, oil, water and coffee essence together, drop into the well and blend into the dry ingredients. Set aside.
Beat the egg whites and cream of tartar in a separate bowl into soft peaks and gradually beat in the remaining sugar until stiff. Fold the egg-white mixture into the flour mixture and blend well together.
Spoon the mixture into an ungreased 20cm (8in) round cake tin and bake in the oven for 40 minutes or until well risen and springy to the touch. Turn the cake out of the tin and leave to cool on a wire rack.
To make the coffee cream icing, beat the vegan margarine until smooth and gradually beat in the icing sugar. Finally beat in the coffee mixture.
Cut the cooled cake in half horizontally and spread half of the icing on the lower half of the cake. Place the top half of the cake back in position over the icing. Spread the rest of the icing on top of the cake and sprinkle with a pinch of coffee powder.

Per serving (for 8): 492 kcals, 32.1g fat, 6.4g saturated fat, 5.2g total protein, 82.5mg calcium, 0.41g sodium

Mung beans in sugar syrup

I love this pudding. It is one of the very few Thai desserts that does not contain coconut milk. Rather than eating it as a dessert, I personally prefer to have it as a snack during the day, perhaps instead of tea and biscuits. A much healthier choice. **Serves 4–6**

225g (8oz) mung beans
1.2 litres (2 pints) water
225g (8oz) brown sugar

Pick out and discard all the coloured and misshapen beans. Wash the beans, cover with warm water and leave to soak for 2–3 hours or, even better, overnight. Wash again and drain before use.

Pour the measured water into a pan and bring to the boil. Add the mung beans and cook over a medium heat for 30–45 minutes until tender and cooked through. The beans will split open once they are cooked.

Add the brown sugar and stir until it has dissolved. Bring back to the boil, then remove from the heat.

Serve cold or hot; I personally prefer it hot.

Per serving: 371 kcals, 0.6g fat, 0.1g saturated fat, 13.5g total protein, 82mg calcium, 0.02g sodium

Candied cassava with soya cream

Cassava is an uncommon ingredient in the west, but you can get it quite easily if you go to the market in an area where there's a large Indian or African population. These people tend to use quite a lot of root vegetables in their cooking. **Serves 4**

300g (10oz) sugar
500ml (17fl oz) water
700g (1½lb) cassava root, peeled, halved lengthways and then cut across into 7.5cm (3in) pieces

For the topping

150ml (¼ pint) soya cream
Pinch of salt

To make the topping, put the soya cream and salt in a small pan and warm over a low heat. Stir constantly to make sure that the salt dissolves completely. Set aside.

Put the sugar and water in a brass or stainless-steel wok and heat over a medium heat. (Cooked Thai desserts are usually made in a brass wok, which does not discolour the ingredients). Gently stir to make sure the sugar is fully dissolved and bring the mixture to the boil.

Reduce the heat, add the cassava pieces and make sure that they are totally covered with the syrup. Leave to simmer for 20–30 minutes or until the cassava is cooked through and has absorbed almost all of the syrup, turning occasionally to make sure the syrup is well distributed among the cassava pieces.

Remove from the heat and transfer to individual serving plates or bowls. Drizzle with the lightly salted soya cream before serving.

Per serving: 611 kcals, 7g fat, 1g saturated fat, 2.2g total protein, 73mg calcium, 0.13g sodium

Watermelon ice

Instead of following the recipe below, if you are in a hurry you can make a lovely frozen drink by blending the watermelon flesh with sugar syrup to taste and some ice cubes together with a small quantity of lime juice and it should give you the same satisfaction! **Serves 4**

100g (3½oz) caster sugar
100ml (3½fl oz) water
500g (18oz) watermelon, plus 4 melon wedges with the rind left on, to serve
2 tablespoons freshly squeezed lemon juice

Put the sugar and water into a pan and heat gently until the sugar has dissolved. Pour into a large bowl and leave to cool.
Cut the melon into wedges and remove the flesh from the rind, discarding the seeds. Cut the flesh into small pieces. Put the melon pieces into a blender and blend until smooth.
Add the cooled sugar syrup and lemon juice to the watermelon slush in the blender and gently blend for a few seconds.
Transfer the mixture into a freezer container and freeze for about 1½ hours. Remove from the freezer and beat the mixture, then freeze for a further 2 hours, beating the mixture at 30-minutes intervals until it has frozen firm.
Transfer the watermelon ice from the freezer to the fridge 20 minutes before it is to be served. Serve in scoops, accompanying each portion with a fresh watermelon wedge.

Per serving: 138 kcals, 0.4g fat, 0g saturated fat, 0.6g total protein, 12mg calcium, 0.01g sodium

Orange soya yogurt ice cream

People on a dairy-free diet who just can't live without ice cream will be delighted to find that this recipe, made with soya cream instead of double cream, works extremely well. It can also be made with lemon or lime juice instead of the orange juice. **Serves 6**

6 tablespoons freshly squeezed orange juice
500ml (18fl oz) soya yogurt
150ml (¼ pint) soya cream
100g (3½oz) caster sugar
Thin strips of orange zest, to decorate

Put the orange juice into a bowl, add the yogurt, cream and sugar and mix well. Then churn the mixture in an ice-cream maker, following the manufacturer's instructions.
If you do not have an ice-cream maker, freeze the mixture in a freezeproof container for 1–2 hours or until it begins to set around the edges. Turn the mixture out into a bowl and stir with a fork or beat in a food processor until smooth. Return to the freezer and freeze for a further 2–3 hours, or until firm. Cover the container with a lid for storing.
Serve the ice cream in scoops, decorated with strips of the orange zest.

Per serving: 175 kcals, 7.9g fat, 0.6g saturated fat, 5g total protein, 4.2g soya protein, 27mg calcium, 0.01g sodium

Chilled cappuccino cups *I was asked to provide a recipe for cappuccino or coffee with soya milk. Well, here is a sophisticated one for you to try. Those who like whipped cream can whip soya cream and put it on top of this chilled coffee pudding before sprinkling with dark chocolate powder.* Serves 4

300ml (½ pint) soya milk
6 teaspoons instant coffee powder
1 egg and 3 egg yolks
125g (4½oz) caster sugar

To decorate
Dark chocolate powder
4 mint sprigs

Preheat the oven to 180°C/350°F/gas mark 4.
Heat the soya milk with the instant coffee powder. Beat the egg and egg yolks with the sugar until well blended. Pour the hot soya milk mixture over the eggs and sugar, constantly whisking.
Place 4 ovenproof coffee cups in a roasting tin. Pour the mixture into the cups. Very carefully pour enough hot water into the tin to come halfway up the outside of the cups. Put the tin in the oven and bake for 30 minutes or until the custards are just set. Remove the cups from the oven, allow to cool, then chill in the fridge for about 1½ hours.
Serve sprinkled with dark chocolate powder and decorated with mint sprigs.

Per serving: 245 kcals, 9g fat, 2.7g saturated fat, 7.2g total protein, 2.2g soya protein, 52mg calcium, 0.05g sodium

Mango smoothie *A smoothie can taste great or not so great, depending on your choice of fruit. You must use at least one fruit that has a dense texture, such as a banana or guava to thicken the drink so that you can avoid using yogurt or cream. You can also substitute the brown sugar with runny honey.* Serves 4

600ml (1 pint) chilled soya milk
200ml (7fl oz) chilled mango juice
2 tablespoons brown sugar
2 ripe mangoes, stoned, diced and frozen
2 bananas, sliced and frozen

Put the soya milk, mango juice and sugar into a blender and blend on a slow setting until well combined. Add the mango and banana chunks and blend until smooth.

Per serving: 220 kcals, 3g fat, 0.3g saturated fat, 5.3g total protein, 4.3g soya protein, 46mg calcium, 0.05g sodium

Lemongrass hot drink *Obviously it's not a requirement that sugar or honey be used in this drink. I personally prefer honey but I also like to add a squeeze of fresh lime or lemon juice at the same time. If you don't like lemongrass, then try making the drink with ginger roots, but omit the citrus.* Serves 4

750ml (26fl oz) water
4 lemongrass stalks, lightly crushed
3 tablespoons light brown sugar or honey (optional)

Bring the water to the boil in a small saucepan over a medium heat. Add the lemongrass, reduce the heat and leave to simmer for 7–8 minutes or until the water begins to turn yellow.
Remove the lemongrass stalks and add the sugar or honey (if using), stirring until dissolved.
Serve the drink hot by itself or with biscuits.

Per serving: 3 kcals, 0g fat, 0g saturated fat, 0.1g total protein, 2mg calcium, 0.01g sodium

Resources

The various dietetic nutrition societies are a good option for getting information about lactose intolerance as well as allergy as they will be able to put you in touch with local groups, and inform you about up and coming events. They also increase awareness within the food industry and lead research into food intolerance. For those with an allergy or anaphalyxis to cow's milk and its derivatives, detail on the issues and risks concerning cross-contamination, food preparation, and eating out is essential. This information is covered in other publications and in fact sheets from an allergy specialist, or support associations such as Allergy UK and the Anaphylaxis Campaign. For anyone looking to exclude dairy from their diet completely for whatever reason you should get an appointment to see a registered dietitian or nutritionist to ensure that you do not miss out on any vital nutrients.

Dietetic and Nutrition Societies and Information Services

UNITED KINGDOM

Allergy UK
3 White Oak Square, London Road,
Swanley, Kent BR8 7AG
Tel: +44 (0)1322 619 898
Allergy Helpline: +44 (0)1322 619 864
www.allergyuk.org

The Anaphylaxis Campaign
PO Box 275, Farnborough GU14 6SX
Tel: +44 (0)1252 542 029
info@anaphylaxis.org.uk
www.anaphylaxis.org.uk

British Dietetic Association
5th Floor, Charles House, 148/9 Great Charles Street, Queensway, Birmingham B3 3HT
Tel: +44 (0)121 200 8080
info@bda.uk.com
www.bda.uk.com

The British Heart Foundation
14 Fitzhardinge Street,
London W1H 6DH
Tel: +44 (0)8450 708 070
www.bhf.org.uk

The British Nutrition Foundation
High Holborn House, 52-54 High Holborn,
London WC1V 6RQ
Tel: +44 (0)20 7404 6504
postbox@nutrition.org.uk
www.nutrition.org.uk

Coeliac UK
PO Box 220, High Wycombe,
Bucks HP11 2HY
Tel: +44 (0)1494 437 278
www.coeliac.co.uk

Food Standards Agency
UK Headquarters, Aviation House,
125 Kingsway, London WC2B 6NH
Tel: +44 (0)20 7276 8000
www.food.gov.uk

H·E·A·R·T UK
7 North Road, Maidenhead,
Berkshire SL6 1PE
Tel: +44 (0)1628 628 638
ask@heartuk.org.uk
www.heartuk.org.uk

lactose.co.uk
5 Crossways Rd, Beckenham,
Kent BR3 3JP
Tel: +44 (0)794 1133 448
info@lactose.co.uk
www.lactose.co.uk

The National Osteoporosis Society
Camerton, Bath BA2 0PJ
Tel: +44 (0)1761 471 771
info@nos.org.uk
www.nos.org.uk

Supermarket Customer Care Lines
Asda +44 (0)500 100 055
Morrisons +44 (0)1274 356 000
Sainsburys +44 (0)800 636 262
Somerfield +44 (0)117 935 9359
Tesco +44 (0)800 505 555
Waitrose +44 (0)800 188 884

The Vegetarian Society
Parkdale, Dunham Road, Altrincham,
Cheshire WA14 4QG
Tel: +44 (0)161 925 2000
www.vegsoc.org

IRELAND

Irish Nutrition & Dietetic Institute
Ashgrove House, Kill Avenue, Dun Laoghaire,
Dean's Grange, County Dublin, Ireland
Tel: +353 (0)1280 4839
www.indi.ie

ITALY

Food Allergy Italia
Piazza De Gasperi, 45/a, Via Paolotti 7,
35131 Padova
Tel: +39 (0)34 0239 1230
www.foodallergyitalia.org

USA

American Dietetic Association
Headquarters, 120 South Riverside Plaza,
Suite 2000, Chicago, IL 60606-6995
Tel: +1 (1)800 877 1600
www.eatright.org

The Food Allergy & Anaphylaxis Network
11781 Lee Jackson Hwy., Suite 160,
Fairfax, VA 22033-3309
Tel: +1 (1)800 929 4040
faan@foodallergy.org
www.foodallergy.org

CANADA
Association Quebecoise des Allergies Alimentaires
5170 Dixie Road, Suite 204, Mississauga, Ontario L4W 1E3
Tel: +1 (1)905 507 6208
www.aqaa.qc.ca

Dietitians of Canada
480 University Ave, Suite 604, Toronto, Ontario M5G 1V2
Tel: +1 (1)416 596 0857
www.dietitians.ca

AUSTRALIA
Anaphylaxis Alliance
21 Robinson Close, Hornsby Heights, NSW 2077
Tel: +61 (0)1300 728 000
www.allergyfacts.org.au

NEW ZEALAND
Allergy New Zealand
PO Box 56117, Dominion Road, Auckland
Tel: +64 (0)800 34 0800
www.allergy.org.nz

SOUTH AFRICA
Allergy Society of South Africa
P.O. Box 88, Observatory, 7935
Cape Town, R.S.A.
Tel: +27 (0)21 447 9019
www.allergysa.org

Dairy-free Products

If you are unable to obtain dairy-free products at your local shop or health food store, contact the manufacturers directly:

UNITED KINGDOM & IRELAND
Alpro UK Ltd
Provamel
Altendiez Way, Latimer Business Park, Burton Latimer, Northants NN15 5YT
Tel: +44 (0)800 018 8180
www.alprosoya.co.uk
Soya milk, yogurt, cream and dessert alternatives and rice milk alternative with calcium

Cauldron Foods
Units 1-2 Old Mill Road, Portishead Business Park, Portishead, Bristol BS20 7BF
Tel: +44 (0)1275 818 448
www.cauldronfoods.co.uk
Tofu specialists

Haldane Foods
Howard Way, Newport Pagnell, Bucks MK16 9PY
Tel: +44 (0)1908 211 311
info@haldanefoods.co.uk
www.haldanefoods.co.uk
Soya milk and meat alternatives

Imagine Foods
Distributed by Kallo Foods Ltd.
Combe Lane, Wormley, Godalming, Surrey GU8 5SZ
Tel: +44 (0)1428 685 100
marketing@kallofoods.com
www.imaginefoods.com/europe
Rice Dream, a low fat alternative to milk made from organically grown brown rice

Plamil Foods
Folkestone, Kent CT19 6PQ
Tel: +44 (0)1303 850 588
contact-us@plamilfoods.co.uk
www.plamilfoods.co.uk
Soya milk, yogurt, cream and dessert alternatives

The Redwood Wholefood Company
Redwood House, Burkitt Road, Earlstrees Industrial Estate, Corby, Northants NN17 4DT
Tel: +44 (0)1536 400 557
info@redwoodfoods.co.uk
www.redwoodfoods.co.uk
Dairy-free 'cheezly' cheese range – supermelting Cheddar, Mozzarella, Edam and Gouda

USA
Devansoy
206 West Seventh Street, PO Box 885, Carroll, Iowa 51401
TEL: +1 (1)712 792 9665
www.devansoy.com
Soymilks and soy flours

Eat In The Raw
PO Box 682, Ashland, OR 97520
Tel: 1 (541) 665 0348
www.eatintheraw.com
Parma-vegan, parmesan alterna-cheese made using only raw organic walnuts, nutritional yeast and Celtic sea salt

Tofutti US
50 Jackson Drive, Cranford, New Jersey 07016
Tel: +1 (1)908 272 2400
Info@tofutti.com
www.tofutti.com
Dairy-free soy product specialists

AUSTRALIA
Sweet William Dairy-Free Chocolate
www.sweetwilliam.com.au

SOUTH AFRICA
South African Soyfood Association
www.soyfood.co.za

Index

Published in 2005 by Angus Books Ltd
12 Ravensbury Terrace
London SW18 4RL

First published in Great Britain in 2005 by
Kyle Cathie Limited

10 9 8 7 6 5 4 3 2 1

ISBN 1 904594 80 8

Editor: Jennifer Wheatley
Series editor: Muna Reyal
Designer: Carl Hodson
Photographer: Martin Brigdale
Home economist: Mini C
Styling: Helen Trent
Copy editor: Ruth Baldwin
Editorial assistant: Vicki Murrell
Recipe analysis: Dr Wendy Doyle
Production: Sha Huxtable and Alice Holloway

A Cataloguing In Publication record for this title is available from the British Library.

Colour reproduction by Colourscan
Printed and bound in Singapore by
Star Standard